Holiday Happenings

by Christal Carter

That Patchwork Place, Inc., Bothell, Washington

Acknowledgments

My thanks to:

My husband, Bill, whose faith and encouragement backed me up.

My daughters, who inspire me endlessly: Carin, who helped so much with the graph work and Catrina, who took over on the home front.

My mother-in-law, Vivian Christiansen, who not only encouraged me, but also did my typing.

My dear friend, Eileen Adams, who told me I could do it.

Nancy Martin and That Patchwork Place for their help and enthusiasm.

And last, but not least, Ruth Briggs, the gracious lady who started it all.

Holiday Happenings©

© 1987, Christal Carter

Printed in the United States of America
93 92 91 90   7 6 5 4

Library of Congress Card Number 86-051627

0-943574-42-0

Preface

My love for the holiday seasons, and the joy and closeness that these times bring, have led me to design the patterns in Holiday Happenings. A special warmth abounds in homes that focus and expand on these wonderful days of celebration. I feel that the carrying on of tradition is especially important in these times of broken homes and single-parent families. Now, more than ever before, it is important to have a reason to come home.

What child wouldn't want to find Valentine placemats with red candles and chocolate hearts when he comes home on a cold February day? Even before I had children, I planned special Valentine's Day dinners for my husband with hand-printed place cards, lace doilies, and heart-shaped cookies. After my daughters were born, they joined the fun and planning of holiday traditions. Each year a collection of "Twas the Night Before Christmas" books sits below a wall quilt with those same words. At Easter, the large "Resurrection" quilt is hung with the Easter egg collection and stuffed bunnies.

I did not want to look back and be sorry for not spending those extra hours to build lifelong memories. And now, with my daughters nearly grown, I have not regretted it. For, wonder of wonders, they don't remember the dusty shelves or fingerprinted windows . . . they talk instead of the tiny biscuits we cut out with thimbles and the miniature cloth doll napkins for tea parties. They reminisce about the Easter egg placemats and bunny salads or the teddy bear Thanksgiving, complete with tiny pies and a roasted cornish game hen.

I hope that you will enjoy these designs for holiday projects and that you, too, will begin building wonderful memories for yourself and your loved ones.

Sincerely,
Christal Carter

Valentine's Day

Christmas Morning

3

Dedication

This book is dedicated to Guy Williams, my father, who taught me not only how to work, but also, how to enjoy it.

The Scent of CHRISTMAS

By Rebecca McPheters

I love the smells of Christmas that abound this time of year:
the smell of cookies baking as mulled cider scents the air;
the smell of turkey roasting and of chestnuts on the fire,
the sound of churchbells tolling as snowflakes frost the spire.

I love the smells of Christmas, when joy perfumes the air—
of John with brown eyes shiny bright and Al with golden hair.
They smell of fresh-scrubbed faces as they tumble into bed,
while thoughts of toys and Christmas plays
        go rushing through their head.

I love the smells of Christmas—the fragrance of the tree,
the scent of fir and pinecones bringing memories back to me:
of Christmas past and present, of a childhood long since passed,
of gifts received and given and of Christmas joys amassed.

Lord, help me give my children that which was given me:
Christmas as a time when dreams came true beneath a tree.
When life was filled with happiness, goodwill was felt by all,
And the house was filled with food and drink
        for friends who came to call.

God bless the Ghost of Christmas Past and may he come again,
to rest in warmth and comfort in the hearts of all good men.
May your Christmas be a merry one, and the New Year happy, too.
May the spirit of this season fill your life the whole year through.

CONTENTS

INTRODUCTION

I was not particularly fond of the Log Cabin design when I first met up with it eight years ago in a beginning quilting class. In fact, I found it boring. I saw the design in every quilting book. The setting diagrams were always the same: Straight Furrows, Streak of Lightning, Barn Raising, or Sunshine and Shadows.

But my teacher insisted we learn the Log Cabin — and learn it I did! Not wanting to make something ordinary, I strove to come up with a design that was different from the usual settings. My first Log Cabin was a star design, and I loved the results. My small 12" x 12" sample grew into a king-sized quilt with several stars and a central spiral design.

I can do more, I thought. I designed a giant Log Cabin butterfly for my daughter's bed. It looked great, won some prizes, and I was hooked on the Log Cabin design possibilities. Since that time, I have made eight large Log Cabin quilts, four Log Cabin crib quilts, and several Log Cabin wall hangings. I have many more designs on paper.

Compared to my large quilts, these holiday designs seem simple. But I think they are whimsical and full of fun, and will allow you to recognize the possibilities in Log Cabin picture designs.

The Log Cabin block, so named because of the "log" strips which compose the block, begins with a central piece, usually a square. Strips are sewn, one at a time, around the central piece. The old, traditional Log Cabin quilts generally had a red or yellow center square, indicating the home hearth, fire, and chimney around which the logs were sewn.

There are actually several blocks that fall into the Log Cabin category. Among them are the Traditional Log Cabin block, Courthouse Steps, and Off-Center Log Cabin blocks. Even the Pineapple pattern is considered a Log Cabin block. The center of the block need not be square. As long as strips are added one at a time to a basic piece (whether it is a triangle, rectangle, diamond, or hexagon), it is still considered to be a Log Cabin block. In my large "Resurrection" quilt I have combined Log Cabin blocks with all of these shapes.

The patterns in this book contain only three types of Log Cabin blocks: Traditional Log Cabin, Courthouse Steps, and Off-Center Log Cabin blocks, all with a square center. I combine the different types of blocks because it greatly enlarges the design possibilities.

Whenever possible in the design, I use Courthouse Steps blocks; they are the easiest and least confusing of all Log Cabin blocks to make. Since these are symmetrical blocks, it is easy to see the placement during piecing.

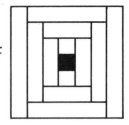

Courthouse Steps Block

The Traditional Log Cabin blocks are a bit more confusing, but they are the only blocks that make a perfect stairstep design, so I use them often. The logs are spiraled, in order, around the central block. In my designs, I keep the center square the same size as my strip width. This gives the "stairsteps" an even appearance. Also, I spiral my Traditional blocks clockwise. All the designs in this book are diagramed that way. If you are used to piecing the Traditional blocks counterclockwise, the diagrams may be confusing to you.

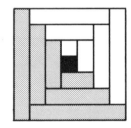

Traditional Log Cabin Block

The Off-Center blocks, which I use rarely, begin with a square piece. The logs, however, are added to two sides only, leaving the center piece bare on two sides. This creates an "off-center" block, which is useful in some designs — the Halloween Jack-O'-Lantern, for example.

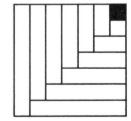

Off-Center Block

I have included templates for several different blocks. Most blocks consist of nine pieces: a central square with two strips on each side. Some blocks consist of thirteen pieces: a central square with three strips on each side.

Occasionally, the pattern will call for a block that is different from all the rest. In those cases, the templates and diagrams, which show an unusual order of piecing, are included. Be aware of those blocks and take extra time and care since they are often confusing.

GENERAL PROCEDURE

Materials and Equipment

Sewing Machine

All you need is one which does a good straight stitch if you are machine piecing. If you plan to machine applique and embroider, you will need a machine with a zig-zag stitch.

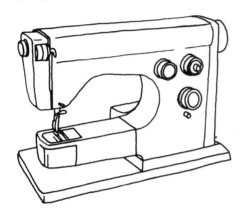

Cutting Tools

Sharp scissors for fabric
Scissors for cutting paper and cardboard
Small embroidery scissors or snips
Rotary cutter and pad (optional, but a real time-saver!)

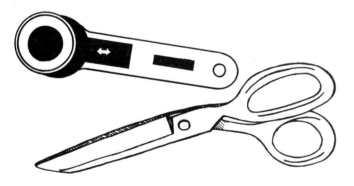

Marking Tools

#2 lead pencils for marking light-colored fabrics
White dressmaker's pencil for marking dark-colored fabrics
Water-soluble fabric marking pens (optional)
Permanent black felt-tip pen for tracing patterns onto tracing paper
Dressmaker's carbon (optional)

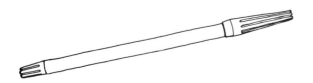

Templates

Clear template plastic, cardboard, or fine sandpaper for making templates
Tracing paper for copying applique patterns
White bond paper for paper-patch method of applique
1" wide linear template for cutting fabric strips if speed-piecing the blocks
Clear plastic ruler

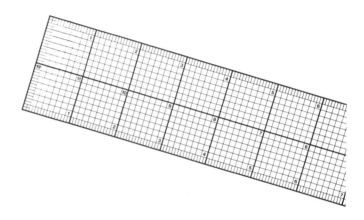

Other Equipment

Light box — wooden box fitted with a clear glass or plastic top and a light underneath, used for tracing purposes. (Make your own by putting a lamp inside a heavy cardboard box and tightly taping glass or plastic to the top — CAUTION: Lamp and cardboard may pose a fire hazard; do not leave unattended; or use a glass-topped table and lamp.)
Iron and ironing board
Hoops — small embroidery hoop
    14"-20" lap hoop for hand quilting
Quilting frame — small adjustable lap-sized frame for hand quilting
Straight pins
Needles — Sharps for applique and piecing
    Quilting needles for hand quilting
    Embroidery needles for embroidery
Thimbles

Other Materials

Interfacing
 Fusible for machine applique
 Nonfusible for "stitch and turn" method of applique
Thread for hand and machine sewing
 Quilting thread for hand quilting
 Embroidery floss
Miscellaneous notions may include buttons, lace, batting, or polyester stuffing.

Fabrics

Fabric Content

As a general rule, 100% cotton fabrics are the best choices for the patterns in this book. The fabrics should be similar in weight and texture, and also colorfast. These will work well for piecing the Log Cabin blocks.

For hand appliqued work, 100% cotton is also preferable. It is easier to work with when folding under the raw edges. If you are not sure of a particular fabric's content, but would like to use it for hand applique, try the following quick test. Tightly pinch a folded edge of the fabric and see if a crease line remains. If a line is plainly visible, the fabric will probably work well for hand applique. If no crease forms and the fabric is difficult to "finger press," it is more likely to be a blend. Blends are more difficult to use for hand applique.

Cotton blends are fine for machine applique, since the raw edges need not be folded under. In fact, a permanent-press blend is often preferred, especially if the finished item will be washed repeatedly. A sweatshirt, for example, will come out of the dryer in great shape if the fabrics used for the applique are blends of cotton-polyester.

I am a firm believer in exceptions to every rule, and since I am not a quilting "purist," I often break the rules. Sometimes I will use silks, satins, velvets, or other specialty fabrics. This can be done with striking effects, but there are many problems involved. Raveling, slipping, stretching, and varying block sizes are some of the problems you will encounter when mixing different textures and weights of fabrics. If you are a beginning quilter, I advise against using these fabrics.

Fabric Preparation

Always prewash and tumble dry fabrics before doing any cutting. Fabrics often shrink or "bleed", even though stated to be preshrunk and colorfast. Even after washing, some dyes continue to bleed, so double-check by pressing a damp corner of the colored fabric onto a scrap of white fabric. If the fabric continues to bleed, try to "set" the dye by adding 1 cup of white vinegar to a sinkful of water and soaking the fabric for several hours. Rinse and test again. If the fabric continues to bleed, discard it. Press the prewashed and dried fabrics before starting to cut.

Fabric Selection

For these Log Cabin picture designs, I use solids, pindots, and small prints that contain few colors. Very busy or large prints tend to complicate the design and draw attention to themselves. It is best if the eye is drawn to the overall picture, rather than a particularly busy or large-print fabric within the picture.

Sometimes I use all one fabric rather than a combination of fabrics. For example, in the "Pilgrims Praying" wall quilt, I used only one white fabric rather then several different whites. The resulting effect de-emphasizes the piecing and creates a unified look to the collars and bonnet.

Too "busy" and confusing

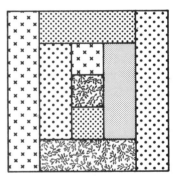

Better choices — more unity, smaller prints

Color Groupings

Deciding how to group the colors is very important. The following exercises will help you learn to group fabrics according to color and intensity (light, medium, and dark).

This type of Log Cabin picture is very different from a traditional Log Cabin pattern or other geometrically pieced design. In these picture designs, especially, you need to achieve unity in color groups. For example, while you may select five different orange fabrics for the the jack-o'-lantern, they need to be oranges that are similar in their intensity (lightness or darkness). They should be all light oranges, all medium oranges, or all dark oranges. Their selection would depend not only on what is available to you, but also, what background selections you have made. The jack-o'-lantern should contrast with the background.

The trick is to use different fabrics to show off your piecing, but fabrics similar enough in color and intensity to form complete and unified objects in the picture.

In the following exercises, cut and paste strips of fabric onto the graphs, using the different two-color combinations suggested. Try to aim for a unified look to each heart, but one that contrasts with the background. Look at the finished samples from a distance. Did you achieve a clear picture of the heart or are there strips that are too dark or too light? Is one of the prints too large or busy? Is the heart distinctively different from the background? Think of these things as you are selecting fabrics for the holiday patterns. Cut sample strips and lay them side by side against a set of background strips. Is there unity and contrast where needed?

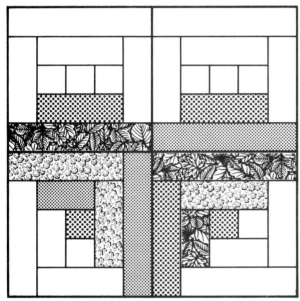

1. Use reds for heart, blues for background.

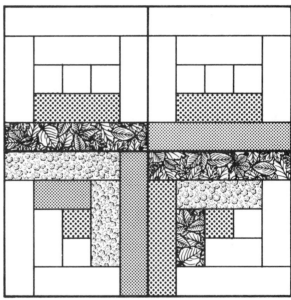

2. Use reds for heart, browns for background.

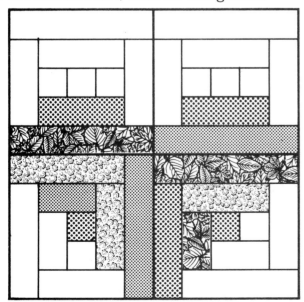

3. Use light browns for heart, dark browns for background.

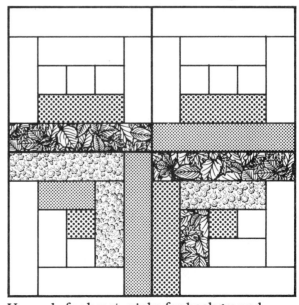

4. Use reds for heart, pinks for background.

Templates

The templates (patterns) on the following pages are shown full size. Be sure to add 1/4" seam allowance to each template. The pieces are numbered to indicate the order in which strips are sewn. Some blocks have nine pieces and some have thirteen pieces, depending on the pattern you are using. Templates should be laid with the long side on the straight grain of the fabric.

Templates may be traced onto graph paper. Be sure to add the 1/4" seam allowance to the graph paper patterns. Before cutting the graph paper, glue the sheet onto a stiff template material: template plastic, cardboard, or the backside of fine sandpaper (the sandpaper side eliminates fabric slippage as you mark). Now cut out the templates very precisely.

Note: If you plan to cut strips for speed piecing, you will not need the templates. All strips will be cut 1" wide. See the Speed-Piecing section on page 14.

Templates for 9-Piece Blocks

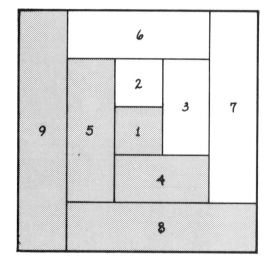

Traditional

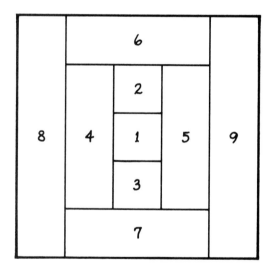

Courthouse Steps

Note: Place long side of template along the straight grain of fabric.

Templates for 13-Piece Blocks

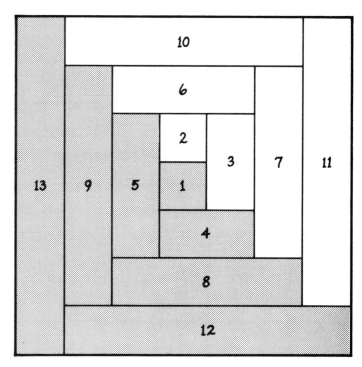

Traditional

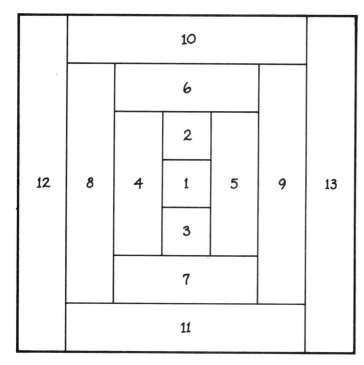

Courthouse Steps

Note: Place long side of template along the straight grain of fabric.

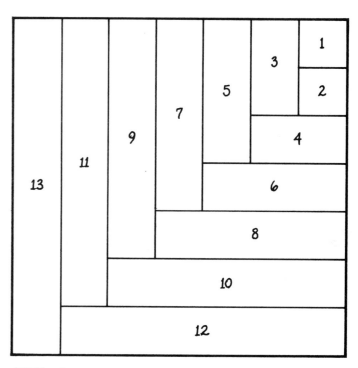

Off-Center

Cutting

There are several fabric cutting methods to choose from. The method you choose depends, in large part, on the piecing technique you select.

If you are using the templates, you will probably use sharp scissors or shears. If you are using fabric strips in a speed-piecing method, you may want to choose a faster cutting technique, such as the rotary cutter and mat. (Some people even use a paper cutter, but I don't recommend it.)

The number one recommendation for cutting with scissors is: use a sharp pair! To cut fabric when using a template, be sure to add 1/4" seam allowance and cut as indicated in the Templates section on page 10.

To cut multiple fabric strips with scissors, lay fabric on a clean, flat surface at a comfortable working height. Fold fabric selvage to selvage. (Although there can be a bit more stretch when the fabric is cut selvage to selvage, I have not found it to be a problem if I cut evenly on the straight of the grain.) If you have very sharp scissors, you may cut up to four layers of fabric at a time (two fabrics folded selvage to selvage). I do not recommend more than four layers; two layers make for more accurate strips. With more traditional size log cabin blocks using 2" wide strips, you can get away with less accuracy, but with the narrow 1" wide strips used in this book, accuracy of width is essential!

Using a linear template 1" wide (or a ruled clear plastic cutting guide), mark the strips 1" wide evenly and accurately across the fabric. Use a #2 lead pencil or a water-soluble fabric marking pen. Use a white dressmaker's pencil for dark fabrics. Make sure pencil tips are sharp to ensure narrow, accurate lines.

To avoid slippage when cutting several layers, you may want to pin the layers together after marking. Try to keep the fabric as flat to the table as possible and cut the strips through all layers.

To use a rotary cutter and mat, follow the manufacturer's instructions. Mats with a premarked grid are especially helpful in keeping the fabric straight.

Lay the mat on a flat working surface at a comfortable height. It is best to stand in order to get the needed pressure for cutting. If you have never used a rotary cutter, spend some time with some scrap fabric or an old sheet and practice! It takes a strong hand to hold the template and apply pressure when cutting, but the results are wondrous! Perfectly cut strips pile up in just minutes.

I often cut up to four layers (two fabrics folded selvage to selvage). There is no need to mark as with scissors cutting; just run the rotary cutter along the template edge. Be sure the template is fairly thick metal or plastic (not wood or cardboard which the cutter will ravage!). Keep fingers well out of the way; the blades are actually round razors and very sharp.

An additional note on the size of the mat for rotary cutting: try to use a mat which is at least 18" x 24". This enables you to fold each fabric in half rather than quarters. I have found that students who use smaller mats or who fold fabric more than once end up with strips that look like the ones illustrated here, because the fabric has not been folded absolutely straight. These zig-zag strips result in irregular blocks.

Folding like this:

Can result in strips like this:

Block Assembly

Sewing Machine

To make quick work of piecing, I use the sewing machine. Before beginning, make sure that your machine is clean and oiled. Replace the needle if necessary.

I set the machine to approximately 12-14 stitches to the inch for piecing. Use matching thread, or, if you are sewing dark fabrics to light, use the lighter colored thread.

Do not change machines during the piecing of a particular project. Even though you may have cut with the same template and set the same 1/4" seam allowance, changing machines often results in varying block sizes. Also, please note that the finished size of your own project may vary slightly from the measurements included here due to varying cutting methods, machines, and even fabric choices. If your machine does not have a seam guide for 1/4" seam allowances, you might want to purchase a magnetized seam guide at your local fabric or quilt shop.

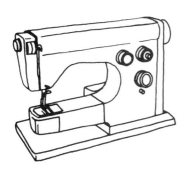

When sewing the completed blocks together, sew the blocks in horizontal rows first. Press seams in row 1 to the right, row 2 to the left, row 3 to the right again, and so forth. Now when you sew the horizontal rows together, match the corners of each block at the seams. They should fit together (snugly) since seams are pressed in opposite directions.

Row #1 - seams to right

Row #2 - seams to left

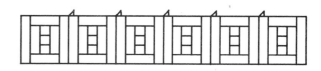

Row #3 - seams to right

Pressing

With such narrow strips in these small log cabin blocks, it is essential to press each log as you go. Make sure there is no fold or tuck in the fabric along the seam, or the log will end up smaller than it should be.

Press both seams to one side. On the Traditional and Courthouse Steps blocks, press all seams away from the center square as shown.

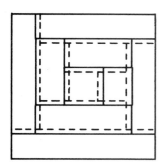

Traditional   *Courthouse Steps*

Wrong sides

13

Speed-Piecing

I speed-piece all of my Log Cabin blocks. All of these patterns use 1" wide fabric strips. Speed piecing is very fast and easy, but there are some basic guidelines to follow.

First, I suggest making a practice block. Cut a 1" square from one of your strips and follow the template guidelines to complete the block. This block will enable you to check seam allowances and finished block size. If you are happy with the results, set it aside to use as a guide for your other blocks.

Basic Guidelines

1. Cut selvages off of strips (I use the selvage as a guide when cutting strips).

2. Strips should be exactly 1" wide, straight, and accurate.

3. Machine stitching should be straight and consistent with 1/4" seam allowances.

4. Strips should be pressed as you sew.

5. When cutting strips (blocks) apart, cut straight and perpendicular to the strip.

Note: This is a very general rule regarding the number of strips to cut: it takes approximately 1 strip 1" wide by 44" long (cut selvage to selvage) to make a 13-piece block. I use the same formula for 9-piece blocks, knowing I will have more than enough strips.

Example: You need to make 12 blocks of dark brown fabrics. If you have 4 dark fabrics, you will need 3 strips of each. (12 divided by 4). If you have 3 dark brown fabrics, you will need 4 strips of each. If you have only 1 dark brown fabric, you will need 12 strips.

This little formula makes it easy to figure yardage. In the above example you would need a total of 12" of fabric or 1/3 yd.

Speed-Piecing Traditional Blocks

The patterns indicate the number of each block type you will need to make. The following sample exercise calls for 6 Traditional blocks:

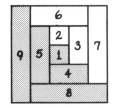

Make 6 Traditional blocks
1/2 browns, 1/2 whites

Look at a Traditional block. The smallest pieces are squares — the center (brown piece #1) and a piece beside the center (white piece #2). Take a strip of brown fabric and a strip of white fabric. Cut them each 8" long (1" for each block needed, plus a couple of inches extra).

With right sides together, sew the strips along one edge using 1/4" seam allowance. Press seam AWAY from the center color — in this case brown. (Reread section on pressing).

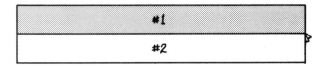

*Seams pressed AWAY
from center square (brown)*

Cut the strip into 6 pieces 1" wide, using your linear template and rotary cutter or scissors. Now you have pieces #1 and #2 sewed together for all 6 blocks.

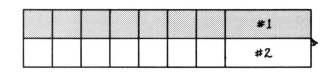

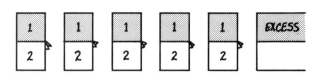

Piece #3 of the sample block is another white. Take a different white strip. Lay this #3 strip on the machine with the right side up.

Note: With speed piecing, the fabric strip ALWAYS goes on the machine first and block pieces are laid on top of the strip.

Place the small block pieces, right side down, on top of the strip. Piece as shown with piece #1 at the top of the strip and piece #2 nearest you. Sew 1/4" from right hand edge of the strip and add block pieces to the strip as you go. If possible, butt the blocks together on the strip. Do not overlap blocks.

Important Note: From this point on, graphs will not indicate color — only the right and wrong sides of blocks and strips. Right side is darkened, wrong side is not.

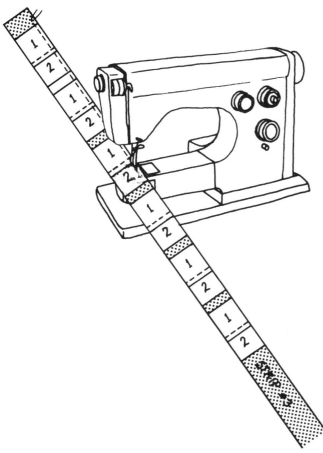

After sewing all 6 blocks to the strip, remove from machine. Cut off excess and cut blocks apart with rotary cutter or scissors. If there is ANY fabric between blocks, cut this out! If small amounts of excess fabric are not removed, blocks will "grow".

Press blocks with seams going away from center. You will now have 6 of these blocks:

Piece #4 is a brown. Choose a brown strip (repeat a fabric if necessary) and place on the machine, right side up.

Note: Remember, these fabrics should be chosen randomly and not sewn in matched order as in ordinary Log Cabin designs.

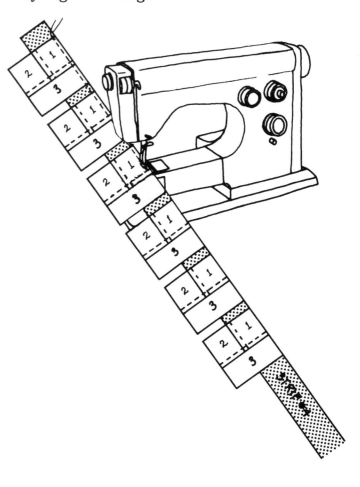

Place blocks right side down on the strip so that piece #3 is nearest you. Always keep the piece that you added last nearest to you as you place it on the strip.

Sew blocks. Remove from machine, cut apart, and press seams away from center.

Repeat this process of sewing blocks to strips until all 9 pieces (or 13 pieces, depending on your pattern) have been added. Refer to the graph regarding piece numbers and colors.

Speed-Piecing Courthouse Steps Blocks

Look at the Courthouse Steps sample block. There are 3 small squares, which are all the same size (pieces #1, 2, and 3). The sample exercise calls for 4, all blue, Courthouse Steps blocks.

Courthouse Steps
Make 4 blocks
All blues

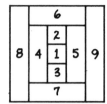

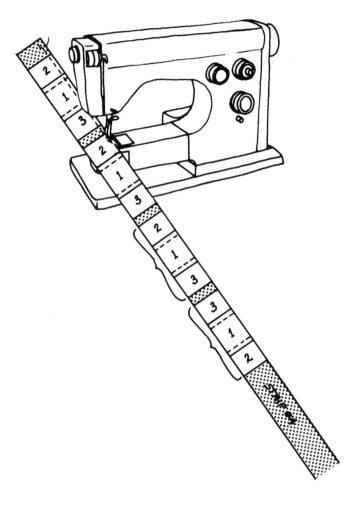

Select 3 blue strips — all different — and cut them 6" long (1" for each block needed plus a couple of inches extra). Sew the 3 strips together as shown and press seams away from center strip.

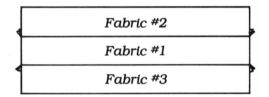

Seams pressed away from center strip

Using 1" wide template, cut strips into 4 blocks.

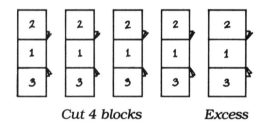

Cut 4 blocks   *Excess*

Now you have pieced #1, 2, and 3 together for all 4 blocks. Select another blue strip for piece #4. (Repeat a fabric if necessary.) Lay the strip, right side up, on the machine. Place the blocks, right side down, on the strip. Unlike the Traditional blocks, you do not place the blocks with the piece you added last nearest you. But with Courthouse Steps, you must remember to lay the blocks so that you will be sewing across a seam.

Blocks may be turned either way on the strip, with piece #2 at the top, or piece #3 at the top. Varying this placement will add more variety to your blocks. Butt the blocks together as you place them on the strip. Do not overlap blocks. Sew along the right-hand side. Remove from machine and cut blocks apart, making sure to cut out excess fabric between blocks. Press seams away from center.

Resulting blocks will look like either of these.

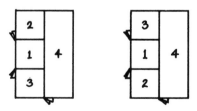

Select a blue strip for piece #5 of the block. Sew blocks onto strip as shown.

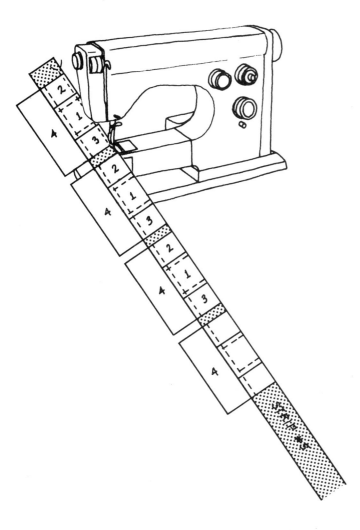

Cut blocks apart and press. Repeat this process of sewing blocks to strips until all 9 pieces have been added (or 13 pieces, depending on your pattern). Refer to graph regarding piece numbers and colors.

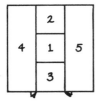

Off-Center or Special Blocks

There are usually only one or two of these blocks in each design, so the speed-piecing method cannot be utilized. Just cut the beginning 1" square (piece #1) from a strip and sew each block individually.

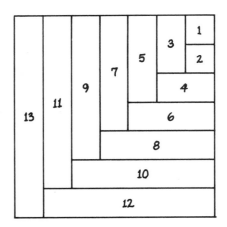

Applique

Applique is the "application" or attachment of a fabric piece to a background fabric. The background may be pieced or it may be one solid piece of fabric.

Applique may be achieved by hand or sewing machine. I have included samples of both in this book. There are various techniques involved in both hand and machine applique. I will discuss just some of these techniques.

In hand applique, especially, I use a variety of techniques. For example, to get perfect circles, I use the paper-patch method of hand applique. This method, though time-consuming, is more accurate. For leaves or flower petals, I might use a simple basted method. Leaves are not necessarily uniform in size and shape, so I save time by eliminating the paper-patch method. Sometimes, for a small, irregular shape that is difficult to work with (a small duck, for example), I use the machine to "stitch and turn" before I applique by hand. So even within one project, I often use a variety of techniques, depending on the pattern, fabrics, and my mood! Use the methods that you find most comfortable for you.

Follow these basic guidelines, however, for all methods:

1. There should be no raw edges showing on the finished project.

2. Light-colored fabrics may need to be lined if darker fabrics show through from underneath.

3. Be sure to add 1/4" seam allowance to all patterns if you are hand appliqueing.

4. If the pattern has arrows to indicate grain lines, place arrows on fabric grain.

Hand Applique — Method 1 — Paper-Patch

Trace the pattern pieces onto a heavy bond paper. Cut out paper patterns. Cut appropriate fabric pieces slightly larger than paper pieces (leave 1/4" seam allowance as shown). Sew a running stitch around edges of fabric and pull taut.

1. Wrong side of fabric goes next to paper.

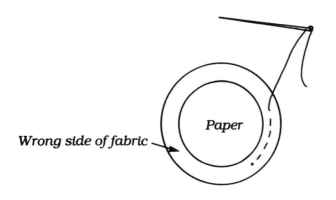

2. Pull stitches taut around paper.

3. Knot end.

Tie a knot and press with paper inside. Applique to background. Slit background fabric behind appliqued piece, being careful not to cut through to front. Remove paper with tweezers.

Hand Applique — Method 2 — Basted

With tracing paper and a permanent black felt-tip pen, trace the patterns from the pattern sheet. (It is best to use a permanent pen so that the traced pattern won't "run" and damage fabric if it accidentally gets damp.) Place the traced patterns on the light box. Using a #2 lead pencil and a white dressmaker's pencil (lead for light-colored fabrics and white for darker ones), trace the patterns and embroidery lines onto the appropriate fabrics. You may also use a water-soluble fabric marking pen, but use only cool water to remove markings. As you mark fabric, be sure to leave 1/4" seam allowance around each piece.

Cut out each piece, adding 1/4" seam allowance to all edges. This 1/4" need not be marked.

Fold the seam allowance to the back on the exact drawn line, but don't let pencil lines show. Using a single basting thread with a knotted end, stitch a row of running stitches around the edges of the folded fabric. I find it helpful to put my knot on the right side of the fabric, so my basting is easy to remove when the applique is complete.

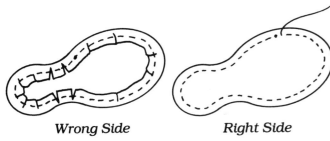

Wrong Side   *Right Side*

Clip curves to fold if necessary.   *No knot needed at end*

Fabric pieces may be pinned or basted to the backing. I only baste if the applique is large or irregular in shape.

To applique, use a small, very thin needle (called a sharp) and a single, matching thread with one end knotted. Use a blind stitch as shown below.

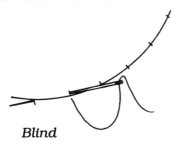

Blind

Hand Applique — Method 3 — Stitch and Turn

This method is helpful to those who feel "all thumbs" when trying to hand applique. It is also useful for small, irregularly shaped pieces. Mark patterns and fabrics as instructed in Method 2, with one exception. Mark fabrics on the wrong side and omit the embroidery lines until later. Cut pieces 1/4" larger than pattern lines indicate.

Use a nonfusible interfacing to back the fabric pieces. Cut the interfacing larger than the cut fabric piece. Place the right side of fabric down on the interfacing and stitch, by sewing machine, around the piece on the solid lines. Cut the interfacing to match the fabric, clipping curves if necessary. Cut a small slash in the center of the interfacing and turn the piece right side out. Press. Mark the embroidery lines, using the light box and applique as instructed in Method 2.

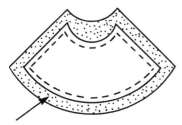

Nonfusible interfacing

Stitch, with machine on penciled stitching line, around entire piece.

Trim interfacing to match fabric piece.

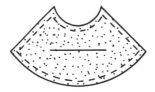

On interfacing side, make a small slit. Turn the piece to the right side through the slit. Press. Mark any embroidery lines and then applique.

Machine Applique

Directions and techniques vary according to the sewing machine used and personal preference. You must have a machine with a zig-zag stitch. Be sure to check your machine handbook for applique instructions. The following are general guidelines.

Before tracing on or cutting fabrics, press fusible interfacing to the wrong side of the fabrics to be used. This prevents stretching and puckering of the fabric pieces. Trace the patterns onto the fabric using a light box or other tracing method. Trace embroidery lines at this time. It is not necessary to add 1/4" seam allowance to pattern pieces since edges are not turned under. Cut fabric on the traced lines.

Pieces may be held or pinned in place, or fused to the background, using a number of commercial products.

The top thread usually matches the fabric to be appliqued. The bobbin thread may be the color of your background or a neutral shade. If the machine is set correctly, this bottom thread shouldn't show from the top.

Use a narrow zig-zag stitch around the piece to hold it in place. Now widen the stitch and do a satin stitch or closed zig-zag stitch around the piece.

Be sure to check your machine manual. It will tell you how to adjust stitches to come to a point (for example at the tip of a leaf) or how to turn a square corner. Some machines have a special foot to attach to enable this heavy stitching to pass smoothly through the feed dog. Some machines have an extra hole in the bobbin, specifically for machine appliqueing and embroidery.

Embroidery

Use good quality embroidery floss and small embroidery needles. The smaller the needle, the finer the stitch you will achieve. Use two threads. (I sometimes use only one for delicate eyelashes and lips or for embroidering letters.)

Make small, accurate stitches, following the appropriate stitch diagrams.

Detached Chain

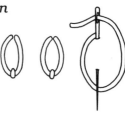

Satin

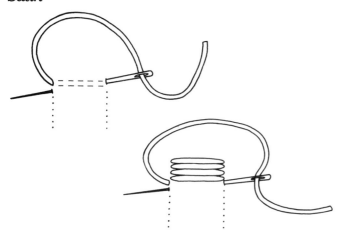

Embroidery Needles

Outline

Straight Stitch

French Knot

HOLIDAY PROJECTS

Nineteen special holiday projects are given in this section of the book. Before beginning a project, read the sections on fabric, tools, and techniques in this book. Then color the picture graphs and blocks for the project you are making.

Fabric requirements and directions are given for each individual project. Where small amounts of fabric are required, 1/8 yd. is listed, since that is the minimum amount of fabric that can be purchased. Don't hesitate to substitute scraps, if you have the appropriate color or print. Use either the full-size templates found on pages 10-11 or the speed-piecing method to construct your blocks.

In several of the projects, special blocks with a different piecing arrangement are used; thus, they do not use the standard templates given on pages 10-11. Full-size templates for these blocks are clearly labeled and found with each individual project.

Strips are often added as borders, once the Log Cabin blocks are joined together. Measurements given are the actual size strip that should be cut; do not add seam allowance.

Applique and embroidery are added when all the Log Cabin blocks are sewn together. Full-size applique patterns, embroidery placement, and directions are printed on the large pull-out pattern sheet.

Finishing techniques for all projects are found in the Finishing section on pages 74-79. These directions provide a variety of ways to finish your projects.

Sweet Valentine Wall Hanging

Approximate Size: 26" x 26" before framing
                              22" x 22" framed on stretcher bar
(Color photo on page 33)

Color Key

☐ - Whites

▨ - Reds

Valentine's Day

Valentine's Day is always special at our house, whether it is a formal dinner in the evening or a simple breakfast before work and school. Valentines, small gifts, and poems are exchanged.

For table decorations, I like to make use of my heart collection. The table may be set with heart-shaped placemats, place cards, and a cut red rose beside each place. For the centerpiece, a cluster of heart-shaped boxes may adorn the table, and to complete the setting, valentine cookies and a heart-shaped teapot!

The Sweetheart Wall Hanging included here is a variation of several I have made, but this one seems especially crisp and fresh with the use of white, red, and green. Hang it for the entire month of February to ward off the chill of winter.

Courthouse Steps Blocks

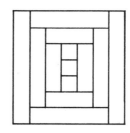 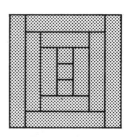

Make 12 blocks.
All whites (background)

Make 6 blocks.
All reds (heart)

Traditional Blocks

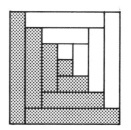

Make 18 blocks.
1/2 red, 1/2 whites
(heart and background)

Sweet Valentine Wall Hanging

Size: 26" x 26"
36 blocks (13-piece blocks)

Materials: 45" wide fabrics
1 yd. red pindot for heart and tulips
1 yd. assorted white prints for background (white background with small red hearts, pindots, or red and green flowers)
1/4 yd. white solid for border
1/8 yd. assorted green fabric for leaves
1/8 yd. assorted red fabric for tulips
3/4 yd. muslin for backing

Notions:
1 yd. each red and green 1/2" wide grosgrain ribbon
1 package (3 yds.) green bias tape for stems
Batting, binding, and thread to finish

Directions:
1. Color in the picture graph and blocks with colored pencils. This will help eliminate mistakes.
2. Using either the speed-piecing method or the templates, make the following blocks:

3. Sew the 36 blocks together as graph indicates. Add 1" wide white print borders to four sides.

4. Applique stems, tulips, and leaves of various reds and greens. Cut bias tape into appropriate lengths for the six tulip stems, using the large graph as a guide to placement. Stems should be appliqued first, then flowers and leaves.

5. Embroider details of tulips in black outline stitch.

6. Sew a 2 1/2" wide white solid border to all four sides.

7. Add batting and backing, then quilt.

8. Add bias binding to finish as a wall hanging or mount on a stretcher bar frame, following directions given in Finishing Techniques section on page 76.

9. Cut red and green ribbon in half. Holding all of the strands together, tie into a bow. Attach bow to tulip stems.

Budding Romance

Approximate Size: 21" x 26"
(Color photo on page 33)

Color Key

☐ - White

▨ - Pinks

▧ - Burgundy or assorted pinks

Budding Romance

Size: 21" x 26"
48 blocks (9-piece blocks)

Materials:
1/2 yd. white fabric for heart
1 yd. assorted pink prints for heart buds, background, and binding
1/3 yd. assorted burgundy prints for heart buds and border
1/8 yd. solid burgundy fabric for heart buds and bow
1/8 yd. green fabric for leaves
2/3 yd. co-ordinating backing fabric

Notions
6 yds. 1/2"-wide ribbon in co-ordinating colors
Embroidery floss — green, black
Batting, binding, and thread to finish

Directions:
1. Color in the picture graph with colored pencils. This will help eliminate mistakes.

2. Using either the speed-piecing method or the templates, make the following blocks:

Courthouse Steps Blocks

Make 24 blocks
All pinks (background)

Traditional Blocks

Make 10 blocks
1/2 white, 1/2 pinks
(heart and background)

Make 14 blocks
White with assorted pinks
or burgundies (heart buds)

3. Set the 48 blocks together as graph indicates.

4. Add a 1" wide border of pink fabric to all sides.

5. Add a 3" wide border of burgundy fabric to all sides. Miter corners if desired.

6. Embroider the stems in green outline stitch, using diagram as guide to placement.

7. Applique 11 green leaves to embroidered stems.

8. Applique burgundy bow to bottom of heart. Embroider bow details with black outline stitch.

9. Mark top for quilting as desired. Layer quilt top with batting and backing and quilt through all three layers. Bind edges with 1 1/2" wide strips of pink fabric. (See finishing instructions on page 75.)

10. Use the remaining fabric scraps in assorted colors to make 4 large stuffed hearts and 2 small stuffed hearts to hang from rod. For each heart:

    a. Cut front and back, then stitch together with a 1/4" seam leaving an opening for turning.

    b. Clip curves and indentation; turn to right side.

    c. Stuff heart firmly; close opening with slip stitch.

11. Stitch a casing to back of quilt (see page 76). Insert a decorative rod. I chose to carry out the Valentine theme by using a wooden rod with heart end pieces.

Sunny Bunny Wall Hanging

Approximate size: 24" x 28"
(Color photo on page 34)

Color Key

☐ - White   ▨ - Pink   ▨ - Yellow   ■ - Black

▨ - Blues   ▨ - Bright pink   ▨ - Brown   ▨ - Green

Easter

As the blossoms of spring appear and Easter approaches, I like to bring out the wall hangings and Easter decorations. Our Easter traditions include an early morning Easter egg hunt, followed by opening the baskets, one for each member of the family. For breakfast we enjoy sweet rolls, sometimes shaped like bunnies or baskets of eggs, and fresh orange juice before the morning church service. For dinner we usually have a leg of lamb and bunny salads, a tradition started by my great grandmother. A pear half, sitting on a bed of lime gelatin grass, forms the body, and almond ears, a miniature marshmallow tail, clove eyes, and a red-hot candy nose complete the bunny. It is not Easter at our house without bunny salads.

I think the spring designs included here are especially fun. The lamb pattern could also be made into a table runner or placemats. Sunny Bunny could be adapted as a baby quilt by substituting flowers or toys for the Easter eggs and enlarging the borders.

Sunny Bunny Wall Hanging

Size: 24" x 28"

72 blocks (9-piece blocks)

Materials: 45" wide fabrics
1 1/3 yds. assorted medium blue prints for sky
1/2 yd. white for bunny
1/3 yd. pink print for inner ears and border
1/8 yd. bright pink solid for cheeks and eggs
1/4 yd. medium brown print for basket
1/8 yd. floral print for bow
1/8 yd. yellow solid for butterfly and egg
1/8 yd. purple print for egg
1/4 yd. green solid for grass, egg, and binding
1/8 yd. black solid for butterfly, nose, mouth
2/3 yd. coordinating fabric for backing

Notions:
Embroidery floss - black, white
Brown bias tape 1/2" wide to match basket (handle)
Batting, binding, and thread to finish

Directions:
1. Color in the picture graphs and blocks with colored pencils. This will help eliminate mistakes.
2. Using either the speed-piecing method or the templates, make the following blocks:

Courthouse Steps Blocks

Make 35 blocks.
Assorted sky blues

Make 5 blocks.
White (ears and face)

Make 2 blocks.
Blues with white
(tips of ears)

Make 2 blocks.
Pink with blue
(ears)

Make 2 blocks.
White with pink
(ears)

Make 2 blocks.
Brown with blue
(basket)

Make 1 block.
center (mouth)
White with black

Make 4 blocks.
Brown (basket)

27

Traditional Blocks

Make 9 blocks.
1/2 white, 1/2 blues
(face and ears)

Make 3 blocks.
1/2 pink, 1/2 white
(ears)

Make 2 blocks.
1/2 white, 1/2 bright pink
(cheeks)

Make 2 blocks.
1/2 yellow, 1/2 blues
(butterfly)

Make 2 blocks.
1/2 brown, 1/2 blues
(basket)

Make 1 block.
1/2 pink, 1/2 blues
(ear)

3. Sew the 72 blocks together as graph indicates.

4. Add 2 side strips of 1" wide blue fabric.

5. Add a top strip of 1" wide blue fabric.

6. Add a 2" wide strip of green to the bottom for grass.

7. Add 2 side strips of 2" wide pink.

8. Add a top and bottom strip of 2" wide pink. Miter corners if desired.

9. Complete applique:

a. Applique brown bias tape handle to top of basket.

b. Applique eggs. Overlap and cut off bottom of eggs so they appear to be inside the basket. Applique bow to handle.

c. Applique bunny's paw to handle.

d. Applique butterfly's body between yellow wings on piecing.

e. Applique bunny nose above mouth section. See graph.

10. Using 2 strands of black embroidery floss and using outline stitch, embroider teeth and upper lip, eyelashes, center of paw, butterfly's antennae, and inner lines of bow. Embroider shine on nose in white satin stitch.

11. Mark quilt top for quilting as desired. Quilting suggestion: Quilt around bunny, basket, bow, eggs, and butterfly; then quilt a grid of horizontal and vertical lines.

12. Layer quilt top with batting and backing and quilt through all three layers. Bind edges with 1 1/2" wide strips of green. (See finishing instructions on page 75.)

28

Lambkins

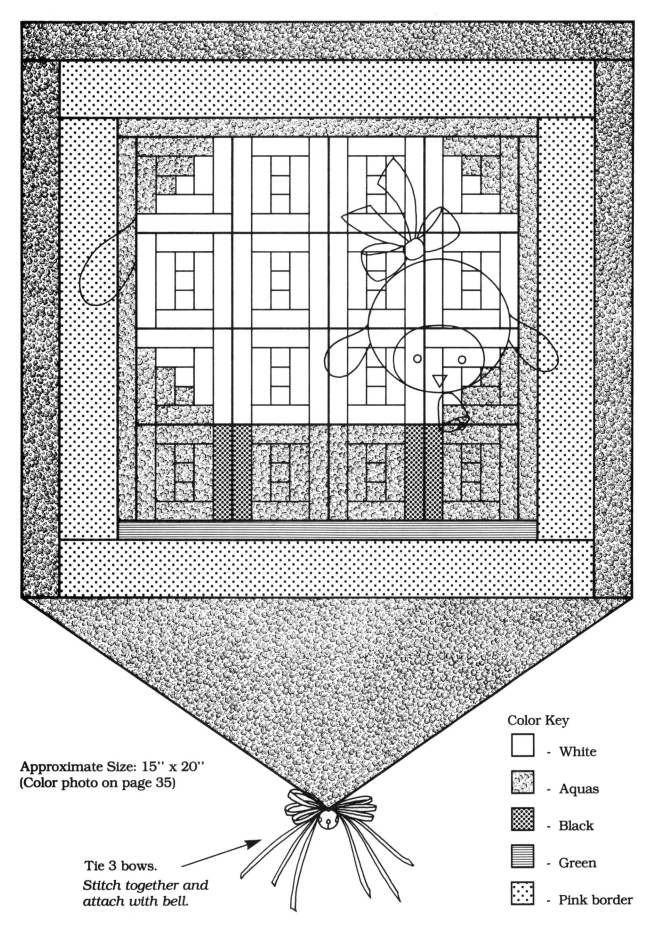

Approximate Size: 15" x 20"
(Color photo on page 35)

Color Key
☐ - White
▨ - Aquas
▓ - Black
▤ - Green
⦂ - Pink border

Tie 3 bows.
Stitch together and attach with bell.

Lambkins Wall Banner

Size: 15" x 20"

16 blocks (9-piece blocks)

Materials: 45" wide fabrics
1/3 yd. white solid for lamb
3/4 yd. assorted aqua for sky and backing (include 1/2 yd. of one aqua for borders, bottom triangle, and backing)
1/8 yd. pink for bow and borders
1/8 yd. gray solid for head
1/8 yd. black print for ears, muzzle, legs, and tail
1/8 yd. gold solid for bell
1/8 yd. green solid for grass

Notions:
Thread
Embroidery floss - aqua, black, pink
Grosgrain ribbon - 1 yd. each pink, aqua, and dark aqua
Bell - 1" wide or smaller
16" x 21" batting

Directions:
1. Color in the picture graph and blocks with colored pencils. This will help eliminate mistakes.
2. Using either the speed-piecing method or the templates, make the following blocks:

Courthouse Steps Blocks

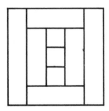 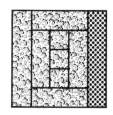

Make 8 blocks.   Make 4 blocks.
All white (lamb)   Aquas with 1 black strip
                       (sky and leg)

Traditional Blocks

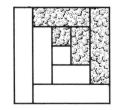

Make 4 blocks.
1/2 white, 1/2 aquas
(lamb and sky)

3. After piecing all 16 blocks, sew them together as indicated in graph.

4. Sew a 1" wide strip of aqua to each side of the block section. Sew a 1" wide strip of aqua to the top. Sew a 1" wide strip of green to the bottom to make grass.
5. Sew pink borders (2" wide) to sides, then top and bottom.
6. Complete all applique and embroidery.
7. Sew 1" wide aqua border to sides and top. For triangle section at bottom of banner, cut a strip of aqua as shown below:

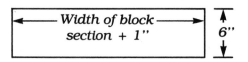

8. Fold this aqua strip in half lengthwise and cut as shown by dotted line.

9. Sew this large triangle to the bottom of banner.
10. Finish banner. Cut a piece of backing fabric slightly larger than banner. Place banner and backing with right sides together. Add a piece of batting underneath.

Layer like this:

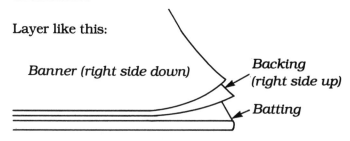

11. Stitch 1/4" inside edge of banner along sides and bottom but leave top open.

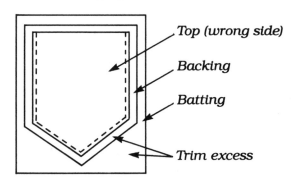

12. Trim excess batting and seam allowances and turn banner to right side. Fold edges of top to inside and slip-stitch closed. Add a back rod casing if desired (see Finishing section on page 76).
13. To trim, add bell and bows as shown.

Spring Chick

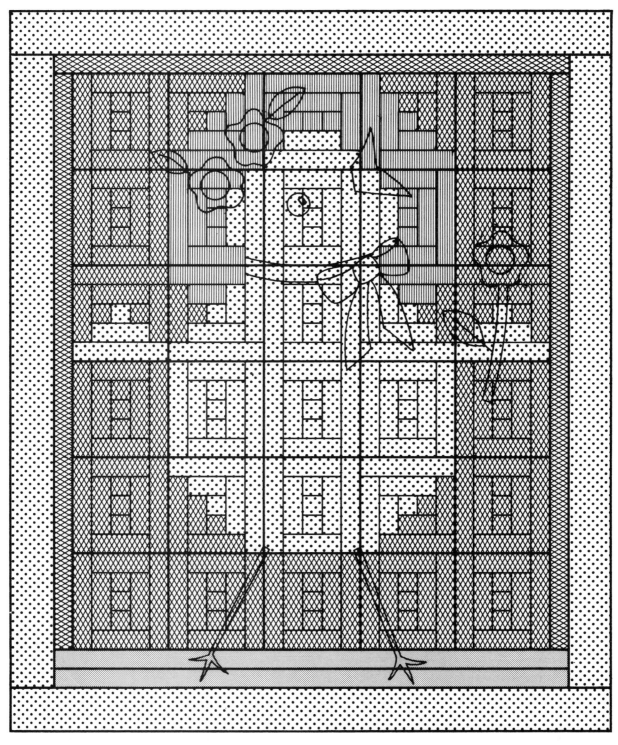

Approximate Size: 17" x 20"
(Color photo on page 35)

(Color photo on page 35)

Color Key

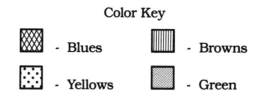

- Blues   - Browns

- Yellows   - Green

31

Spring Chick Wall Hanging

Size: approximately 17" x 20"
30 blocks (9-piece blocks)

Materials: 45" wide fabrics
1/8 yd. each of 4 similar blue fabrics for sky
1/2 yd. each of 4 similar yellow fabrics for chick, border, and binding
1/8 yd. brown for bonnet
1/8 yd. green solid for grass and leaves
1/8 yd. pink print for bow and flowers
1/8 yd. orange print for beak
1/8 yd. black for eyes
1/2 yd. coordinating color for backing fabric

Notions:
Embroidery floss - black, white, orange
Green bias tape - small scrap for flower stem
Batting, binding, and thread to finish

Directions:
1. Color in the picture graphs and blocks with colored pencils. This will help eliminate mistakes.
2. Using either the speed-piecing method or the templates, make the following blocks:

Courthouse Steps Blocks

Make 13 blocks.
All blue (sky)

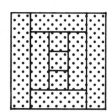

Make 6 blocks.
All yellows (chick)

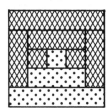

Make 2 blocks.
Blues with yellow
(wings)

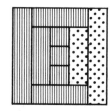

Make 3 blocks.
Brown with yellow
(bonnet and head)

Traditional Blocks

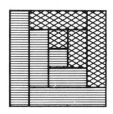

Make 2 blocks.
1/2 browns, 1/2 blues
(bonnet and sky)

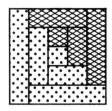

Make 2 blocks.
1/2 yellows, 1/2 blues
(chick and sky)

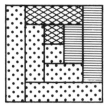

Make 1 block.
1/2 yellows with brown and blue (chick, sky, and bonnet)

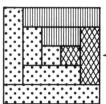

Make 1 block.
1/2 yellows with brown and blue (chick, sky, and bonnet)

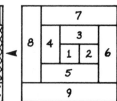

Note: This is an unusual block. Numbering sequence is reverse of normal.

3. Sew the 30 blocks together as graph indicates.
4. Add 2 side strips of 1" wide blue fabric. Add a top strip of 1" wide blue fabric.
5. Add 2 green 1" wide strips to the bottom for grass.
6. Add 2 side border strips of 2" wide yellow fabric. Add top and bottom border of 2" wide yellow fabric.
7. Complete applique:

   a. Applique neckband and bow of pink fabric to chick's neck.

   b. Applique orange beak and black eye to head.

   c. Applique flower stem of green bias tape.

   d. Applique pink flowers to bonnet and stem.

   e. Applique green leaves to bonnet and stem.

   f. Applique yellow centers to flowers.

8. Complete embroidery:

   a. Embroider leaf veins and inner bow lines in black outline stitch.

   b. Embroider white "sparkle" in chick's eye using satin stitch.

   c. Embroider chick's legs and feet using several parallel rows of orange outline stitch.

9. Mark quilt top for quilting as desired. Quilting suggestion: Outline chick, then quilt sky area in squares.

10. Layer quilt top with batting and backing and quilt through all three layers. Bind edges with 1 1/2" wide strips of yellow. See finishing instructions on page 75.

Budding Romance (above) 21" x 26", features heart-shaped flowers inside a white heart. Stuffed hearts hanging from a decorative dowel add a finishing touch to this romantic theme.

The Sweet Valentine Wall Hanging (left) 22" x 22", decorates a Valentine tea party, complete with heart-shaped teapot. Hang this fresh white, red and green wall hanging for the entire month of February to ward off the winter chill.

Sunny Bunny Wall Hanging, 24'' x 28'', brightens Easter morning with its gay pastel colors. Behind the door, we see the Easter Bunny has left a special basket.

Welcome spring with these decorative banners. **Lambkins** (above), 15" x 20", is adorned with gay ribbons and a bell. **Spring Chick** (left) 17" x 20", shows off her festive Easter bonnet.

The Star-Spangled Flag Quilt, 25" x 40", and pillow, 16" x 16", set the theme for this Independence Day picnic. The wave quilting design adds movement to the flag.

Star-Spangled Flag Quilt

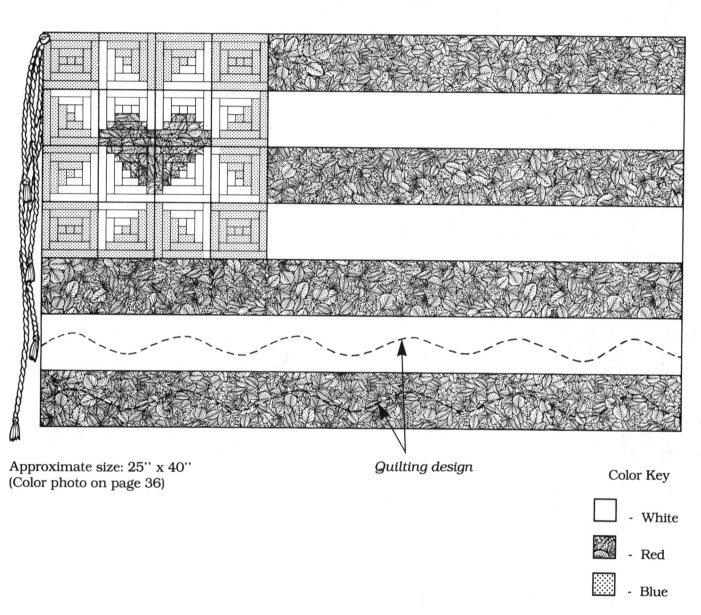

Approximate size: 25" x 40"
(Color photo on page 36)

Quilting design

Color Key

☐ - White

▨ - Red

⬚ - Blue

Independence Day

Fireworks are prohibited in the hills of Southern California where we make our home, so we celebrate by flying flags of all sizes. We like to invite scores of friends and relatives for an old-fashioned picnic with hot dogs, baked beans, watermelon, and other traditional foods.

To decorate the inside of the house last year, I arranged our collection of teddy bears in a parade across the stone hearth. Each carried a miniature flag or a red balloon. On the wall, above the parade, hung the new Star-Spangled Flag Quilt.

Courthouse Steps Blocks

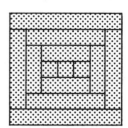

Make 4 blocks.
All blues
(background)

Star-Spangled Flag Quilt

Size: 25" x 40"
16 blocks (13-piece blocks)

Materials: 45" wide fabrics
1/3 yd. assorted royal blue prints for background
2/3 yd. white or muslin solid for stars and stripes
2/3 yd. red print for heart, stripes, and binding
3/4 yd. coordinating fabric for backing

Notions:
Batting, binding, and thread to finish
3 yds. red, white, or blue braided cord

Directions:

1. Color in the picture graphs and blocks with colored pencils. This will help eliminate mistakes.

2. Using either the speed-piecing method or the templates, make the following blocks:

Traditional Blocks

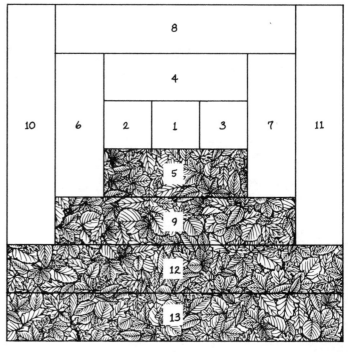

Make 2 blocks.
White with red
(top of heart)

Note unusual piecing; use full-size templates provided here.

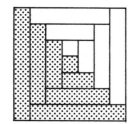

Make 8 blocks.
1/2 blues, 1/2 white
(tips of star)

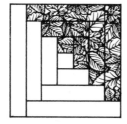

Make 2 blocks.
1/2 white, 1/2 red
(bottom of heart)

3. Before sewing blocks together, measure 1 block. (It should be close to 4" square from raw edge to raw edge.)

The stripes for the flag will be cut the same width as your blocks. If blocks are 3 3/4" wide, cut strips 3 3/4" wide. If blocks are 4 1/4" wide, strips should be 4 1/4" wide.

Cut the following strips, using the width of your blocks as the width:
2 white strips - 26" x block width
1 white strip - 40" x block width
2 red strips - 26" x block width
2 red strips - 40" x block width

4. Sew the 16 blocks together along with the strips as shown:

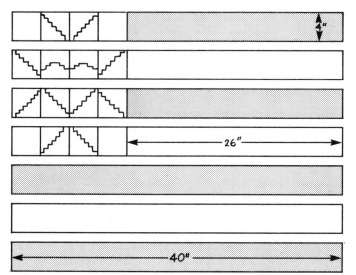

5. Then, matching seams of blocks, sew the 7 linear strips together to form flag.
6. Mark quilt top for quilting. Quilting suggestion: Quilt around heart and star. Quilt "waves" along the stripes.

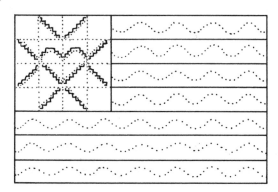

7. Layer quilt top with batting and backing. Quilt through all three layers. Bind with 1 1/2" wide strips of red. See finishing instructions on page 75.

8. Cut braided cord into 2 unequal lengths. Tie knots at ends, fold, and sew to upper left-hand corner of flag quilt.

Star-Spangled Pillow

Size: 16" x 16" (or larger if desired)
(Color photo on page 36)
16 blocks (13-piece blocks)

Materials: 45" wide fabrics
1/3 yd. assorted royal blue prints for background
1/3 yd. white or muslin solid for star
5/8 yd. red print for heart, backing, and binding

Notions:
Thread
2 yds. cable cording
16" x 16" or larger pillow form

Directions:

1. Color in the picture graph and blocks with colored pencils. This will help eliminate mistakes.

2. Using either the speed-piecing method or the templates, make the blocks as indicated in the Star-Spangled Flag Quilt.

3. Sew the 16 blocks together as graph indicates.

4. Add royal blue borders to all four sides of block section. Adjust size of border strips to fit the size of pillow you select. (Pillow must be at least 16" x 16".) For a 16" x 16" pillow, border strips should be cut 1" wide.

5. Finish as a corded pillow, following directions on page 77.

Note: Adjust size of borders to fit your particular pillow form. For 16" square side, strips should be about 1" wide.

"Bootiful" Friends Wall Hanging

Approximate Size: 24" x 31"
(Color photo on page 45)

Color Key

☐ - Whites   ▦ - Oranges

⊡ - Grays   ▨ - Blacks

40

Halloween

Halloween time at our home finds me under the giant California oaks, collecting acorns and dried branches, or in the nearby mountains picking up bushels of pine cones. I then arrange all of these autumn decorations on the porches or patio. Using large oak barrels, buckets, and tubs to pile high my October treasures, I add gourds, pumpkins, and Indian corn for color.

The small wall quilts which are included here have been designed to be whimsical and fun, so that even small children will not be frightened by them. Instead of the Jack-o'-lantern Placemats, you can make a table runner using the pattern on page 71, substituting the pumpkin for the wreath.

"Bootiful" Friends Wall Hanging

Size: 24" x 31"
88 blocks (9-piece blocks)

Materials:
1 1/4 yd. white prints and solids for ghost
1 yd. gray prints for background
1/2 yd. orange prints for pumpkin, floor, and binding
3/4 yd. black prints for cat, bow tie, spider, eyes, mouth, stem, and border
  Note: Include 1/4 yd. of one of the blacks to insure enough for the border.
1/8 yd. yellow print for cat's bow and pumpkin's face
3/4 yd. coordinating backing fabric

Notions:
Embroidery floss: black, white, green, orange
Batting, binding, and thread to finish

Directions:
1. Color in the picture graphs and blocks with colored pencils. This will help eliminate mistakes.
2. Using either the speed-piecing method or the templates, make the following blocks:

Make 5 blocks.
All oranges
(pumpkin)

Make 1 block.
Black and white
(bow tie)

Make 1 block.
Grays with
black center
(spider)

Make 1 block.
Black and whites
(cat's face)

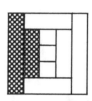

Make 1 block.
Mostly blacks with
some whites (cat's
back and head)

Make 1 block.
All whites with
1 black strip
(cat's tail)

Courthouse Steps Blocks

Make 40 blocks.
All whites
(ghost)

Make 19 blocks.
All grays
(sky)

Traditional Blocks

Make 12 blocks.
1/2 grays, 1/2 whites
(sky and ghost)

Make 4 blocks.
1/2 grays, 1/2 oranges
(sky and pumpkin)

Full-Size Templates for Special 9-Piece Blocks

Make 1 block each:

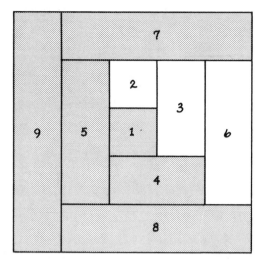

Black and white   (cat's back and tail)

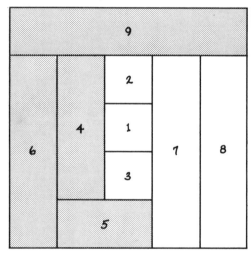

Black and white   (cat's paw)

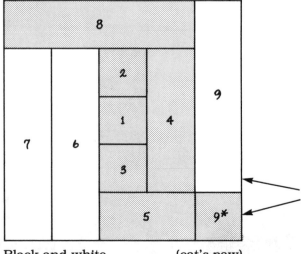

Black and white   (cat's paw)

3. After all 88 blocks are completed, assemble as shown in diagram.

4. Add side strips (1" wide gray) and a top strip (1" wide gray). Add a bottom strip of "floor" (1" wide orange). Then, using black strips 2" wide, add a border to all four sides.

5. Complete applique and embroidery:

a. Applique ghost's eyes and mouth, not centered, but tipped slightly sideways as shown.

b. Eyelashes are black outline stitch and gleam in eyes is a white satin stitch. The grin lines at mouth corners are black outline stitch.

c. Applique yellow eyes, nose, and mouth to pumpkin.

d. Applique black stem and black of eyes to pumpkin. Eyelashes are embroidered in black outline stitch and gleam in eyes is white satin stitch.

e. Applique yellow bow to cat's tail. The details of the bow are in black outline stitch.

f. The cat's ears are several rows of black outline stitch. The eyes are embroidered in green satin stitch with black satin stitch irises. The nose and mouth are white outline stitch.

g. Cat's claws are a black straight stitch. The spider web is a black outline stitch.

h. The 8 spider legs are in black outline stitch with orange detached-chain stitch shoes. The spider's head is a black satin stitch with orange eyes and nose in French knots.

6. Mark quilt as desired for quilting. Quilting suggestion: Quilt around all of the objects (ghost, cat, spider, and pumpkin), and then quilt a series of squares within the ghost. For background, follow the ghost's shape around the outside.

7. Layer quilt top with batting and backing. Quilt through all three layers. Bind with 1 1/2" wide strips of orange fabric. (See finishing instructions on page 77.)

On the last 2 Courthouse Steps blocks (cat's paws in blacks and whites), please note the strip sequence is abnormal. The last block (*) has special piecing of strip #9 before it is added to block.

Sew 2 pieces together first, then add as strip #9.

Jack-O'-Lantern Sweatshirt, Placemat, or Trick-or-Treat Bag

Sweatshirt, Placemat, or Trick-Or-Treat Bag
Size: 12" x 12" (pieced jack-o'-lantern only)
9 blocks (13-piece blocks)

Materials: 45" wide fabrics
1/3 yd. assorted orange prints for jack-o'-lantern
1/4 yd. assorted gray prints for background
1/8 yd. yellow solid for eyes, nose, and mouth
1/8 yd. light brown for stem
1/8 yd. dark brown print for mouse
Scrap of black fabric for eyes
* Additional fabrics may be needed, depending on the project you choose. These additions are noted under each project.

Notions:
Embroidery floss - white
Thread

To decorate as a sweatshirt:
Sweatshirt - purchased or sewn
1/2 yd. fusible (iron-on) interfacing

To finish as a trick-or-treat bag:
1 yd. print fabric for bag back, lining, and handles
1/8 yd. orange fabric for border around jack-o'-lantern
9" x 20" fusible interfacing for handles
13" x 13" batting for bag front

To finish as a placemat: (Yardage given is for one placemat only; multiply all amounts by the number of mats needed.)

3/4 yd. gray print for placemat back, side strips, and binding.

13" x 16" batting

Note: Add extra fabric if you wish to make matching napkins (15" x 15" square for each napkin).

Directions:

1. Color in the picture graphs with colored pencils. This will help eliminate mistakes.

2. Using either the speed-piecing method or the templates, make the following blocks:

Note: Unless you are making several jack-o'-lanterns, it will be difficult to use the speed-piecing method, since there are several "one-of-a-kind" blocks.

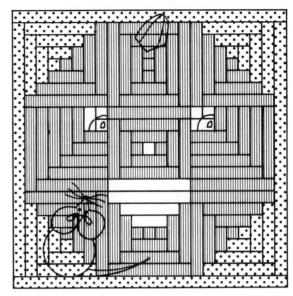

Approximate Size: 12" x 12"
(Color photo on page 45)

Color Key

- Grays

- Oranges

- Yellow

Stem

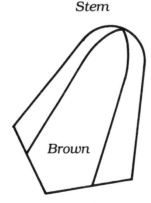

Brown

Eye

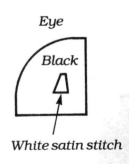

Black

White satin stitch

43

Courthouse Steps Blocks

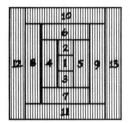

Make 1 block.
All oranges
(pumpkin)

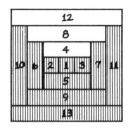

Make 1 block.
Oranges and yellow
(mouth)

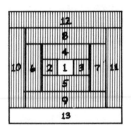

Make 1 block.
Yellow side strip,
yellow center, the rest
oranges (nose and mouth)

Traditional Blocks

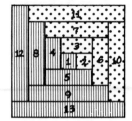

Make 4 blocks.
1/2 oranges, 1/2 grays
(pumpkin and
background)

Full-Size Template
Off-center block

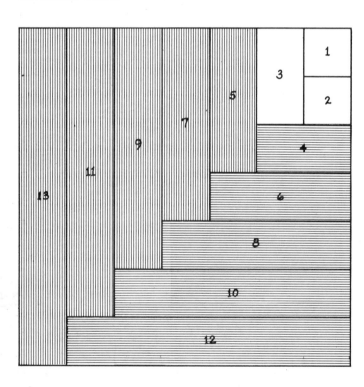

Make 2 blocks.
Pieces 1, 2, and 3 are
yellow (eyes); the rest are oranges

3. Sew the 9 blocks together as graph indicates.

4. Add 2 side strips of 1" wide gray fabric. Add a top and bottom strip of 1" wide gray fabric.

5. Applique the mouse, eyes, and pumpkin stem by hand or machine. Sample shown is machine appliqued. (Patterns for eyes and pumpkin stem are on page 43; mouse pattern is on page 51.)

6. Embroider mouse's eyes and ear details. Sew small yellow bows to mouse's tail and pumpkin stem; if you are making placemats, omit the bows.

7. Finish as sweatshirt (see page 79), placemat (see page 79), or trick-or-treat bag (see page 78).

8. Finish napkins using directions on page 79.

"Bootiful" Friends (above), 24" x 31", hangs on the door to welcome trick-or-treaters wearing **Jack-O-Lantern Sweatshirts.** All the goodies are carried in a **Cat Trick-or-Treat Bag.** Inside the house, **Cat Placemats with Mouse Napkins** are part of the Halloween party decorations.

The Praying Pilgrims Wall Quilt (above) 26" x 34", expresses Thanksgiving sentiments. Hang it near a Thanksgiving table set with **Turkey Placemats** and **Pumpkin Napkins** (right).

The Indian Corn Wall Hanging (left) 24" x 34", will be a welcome decoration all through the fall months. Serve Christmas dinner on a table adorned with the **Wreath Table Runner** (below) and Christmas tree plates.

Santa left a generous amount of gifts in the large **Reindeer and Snowman Stockings,** 15'' x 17''. A **Jolly Santa Wall Hanging,** 20½'' x 20½'', hangs above the fireplace.

The wreath design from the **Wreath Table Runner** has been adapted to a wall hanging and ruffled pillow while the **Reindeer Stocking** has been adapted to a whimsical wall hanging. Use the Finishing Techniques on pages 74 to 79 to adapt designs to various projects. The smaller pieced motifs can be used interchangeably in pillows, placemats, tote bags, or small wall hangings.

Cat Placemat or Trick-or-Treat Bag

Size: 15" x 15"
(Color photo on page 45)

9 blocks (13-piece blocks)

Materials: 45" wide yardage
1/3 yd. black prints for cat
1/3 yd. gray prints for background
1/8 yd. orange fabrics for cat's ears, nose, and bow
1/8 yd. light gray solid for mouse
1/8 yd. green for cat's eyes

Notions:
Embroidery floss - black, white, gray, and orange
Thread

To finish as a trick-or-treat bag:
1 yd. print fabric for bag back, lining, and handles
1/8 yd. orange print for border around pieced cat
Fusible interfacing for handles (9" x 20" piece)
16" x 16" batting for bag front

To finish as a placemat:
(Yardage given is for one placemat only; multiply fabric amounts by the number of placemats needed.)
3/4 yd. gray print fabric for placemat back, side
   strips, and binding
15" x 18" batting

For napkins:
Allow a 15" square of fabric for each napkin.

Directions:
1. Color in the picture graphs and blocks with colored pencils. This will help eliminate mistakes.
2. Using either the speed-piecing method or the templates, make the following blocks:

Courthouse Steps Blocks

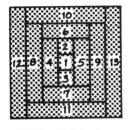

Make 5 blocks.
All blacks (cat)

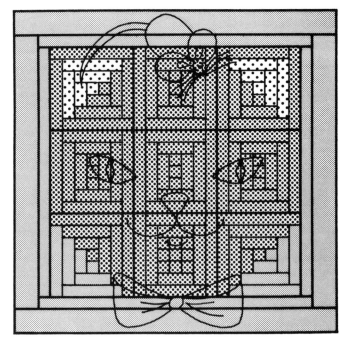

Pieced cat section

Color Key

 - Blacks

 - Oranges

 - Medium grays

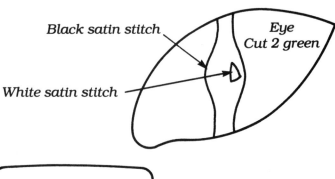

Black satin stitch

White satin stitch

Eye
Cut 2 green

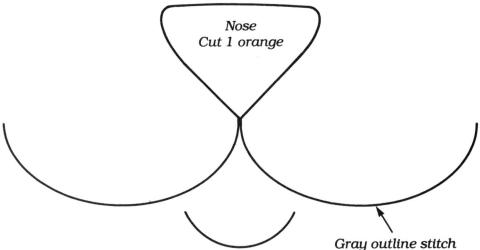

Nose
Cut 1 orange

Gray outline stitch

50

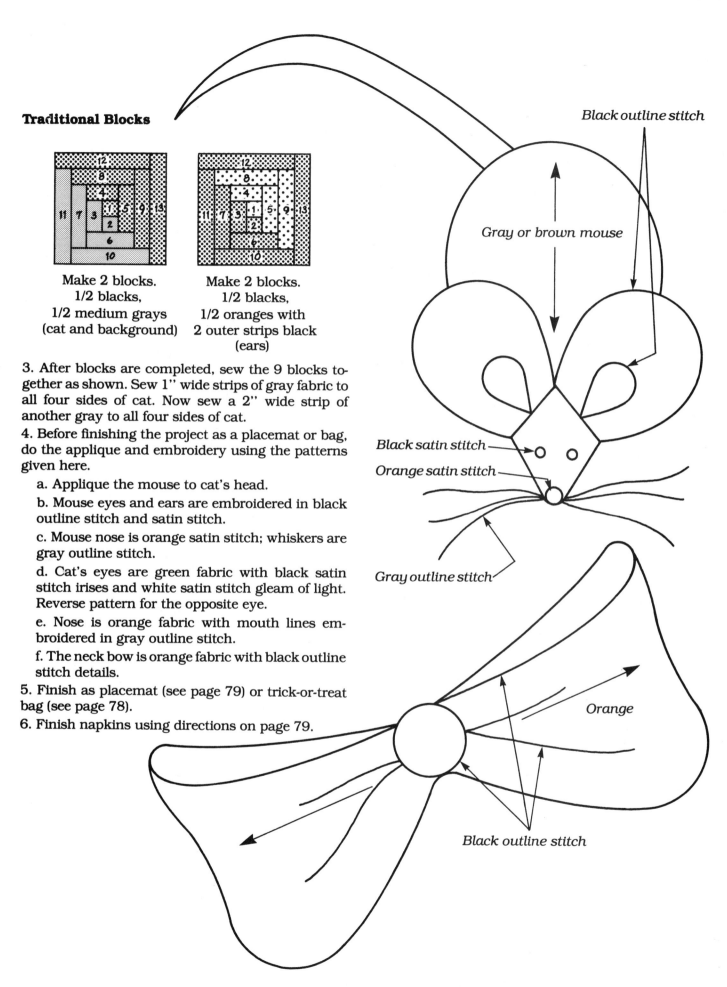

Traditional Blocks

Make 2 blocks.
1/2 blacks,
1/2 medium grays
(cat and background)

Make 2 blocks.
1/2 blacks,
1/2 oranges with
2 outer strips black
(ears)

3. After blocks are completed, sew the 9 blocks together as shown. Sew 1" wide strips of gray fabric to all four sides of cat. Now sew a 2" wide strip of another gray to all four sides of cat.

4. Before finishing the project as a placemat or bag, do the applique and embroidery using the patterns given here.

a. Applique the mouse to cat's head.

b. Mouse eyes and ears are embroidered in black outline stitch and satin stitch.

c. Mouse nose is orange satin stitch; whiskers are gray outline stitch.

d. Cat's eyes are green fabric with black satin stitch irises and white satin stitch gleam of light. Reverse pattern for the opposite eye.

e. Nose is orange fabric with mouth lines embroidered in gray outline stitch.

f. The neck bow is orange fabric with black outline stitch details.

5. Finish as placemat (see page 79) or trick-or-treat bag (see page 78).

6. Finish napkins using directions on page 79.

Black outline stitch

Gray or brown mouse

Black satin stitch

Orange satin stitch

Gray outline stitch

Orange

Black outline stitch

Praying Pilgrims

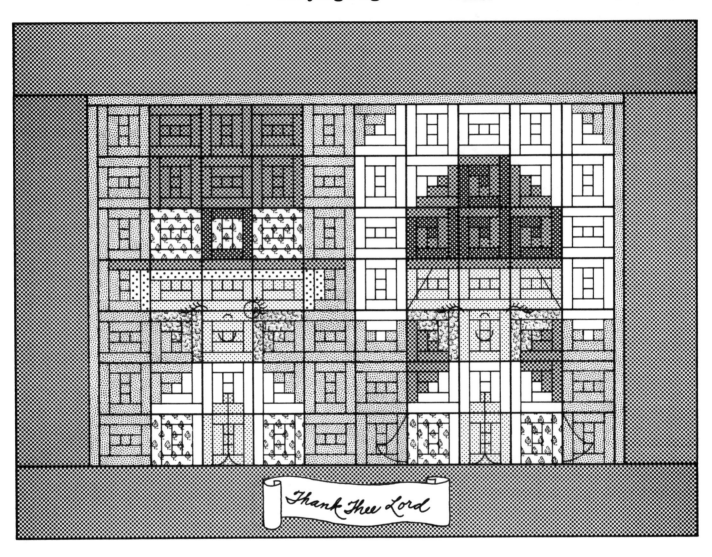

Approximate Size: 26" x 34"
(Color photo on page 46)

Color Key

☐ - White

▫ - Blues

▨ - Beiges

▦ - Browns

▨ - Yellows

■ - Black

▫ - Flesh

▨ - Bright pink

Thanksgiving

Even though there is no snow in Valley Center, it does get quite cold. When the autumn air turns snappy, I like to hang Indian corn in beribboned clusters from the doors. This tradition inspired me to make the Indian Corn Wall Hanging included here.

Last year, to add a new twist to our traditional Thanksgiving dinner, I prepared a feast for the members of our teddy bear collection. A small table was set with tiny candles, place cards, china, and a miniature bouquet centerpiece, and the teddies, with napkins tucked under their chins, were seated around it. Real food, with three different kinds of miniature pies, a batch of tiny biscuits (cut with a thimble), even little after-dinner mints, adorned the table, and in the oven a tiny cornish game hen roasted alongside our twenty-pound turkey!

The bears were the highlight of the conversation as we dined on our new Turkey Placemats and sat beside the Praying Pilgrims Wall Hanging.

Praying Pilgrims Wall Hanging

Size: 26" x 34"
70 blocks (9-piece blocks)

Materials: 45" wide fabrics
3/4 yd. white solid for bonnet, collars, cuffs, and
　scroll
2/3 yd. assorted blue prints for sky
1/2 yd. assorted beige prints for sleeves, hatband,
　and binding
1 yd. assorted brown prints for hat, hair, and border
　(Include at least 1/2 yd. of one of the browns for
　border.)
1/8 yd. assorted yellow prints for boy's hair
1/8 yd. black print for buckle and girl's curls
1/4 yd. flesh fabric for hands and faces
1/8 yd. bright pink fabric for cheeks
1 yd. coordinating backing fabric

Notions:
Embroidery floss - brown, dark pink, and white
2 dark brown or black buttons for boy's cuffs
1/2 yd. 3/8" wide yellow grosgrain ribbon for bow
1/4 yd. 3/8" wide beige lace for girl's cuff
Batting, binding, and thread to finish

Directions:

1. Color in the picture graphs and blocks with colored pencils. This will help eliminate mistakes.
2. Using either the speed-piecing method or the templates, make the following blocks:

Courthouse Steps Blocks

Make 16 blocks.
All blues (sky)

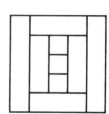

Make 9 blocks.
White (bonnet)

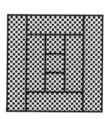

Make 6 blocks.
All browns
(hat)

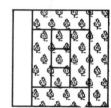

Make 4 blocks.
Beiges with 1 white strip
(arms and cuffs)

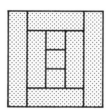

Make 4 blocks.
All flesh
(faces and hands)

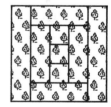

Make 2 blocks.
All beiges
(hatband)

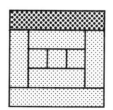

Make 3 blocks.
Flesh with 1 brown strip
(girl's face and bangs)

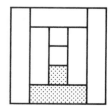

Make 2 blocks.
White and flesh
(tops of hands)

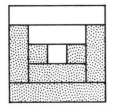

Make 2 blocks.
Blues and white
(sky and bonnet)

Make 1 block.
Beige with black
(boy's hat, buckle)

Full-Size Templates

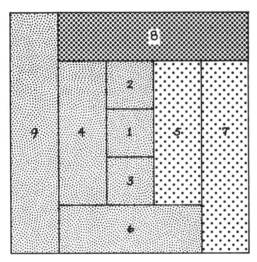

Make 1 block.
Blues with yellows and brown
(sky, boy's hair, and hat brim)

* Note unusual piecing.

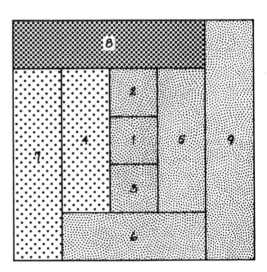

Make 1 block.
Blues with yellows and brown
(sky, boy's hair, and hat brim)

* Note unusual piecing.

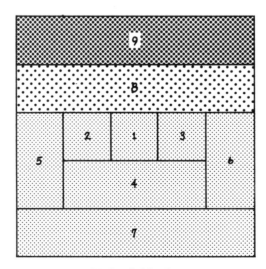

Make 3 blocks.
Flesh with yellow and brown
(boy's face, hair, and hat brim)

* Note unusual piecing.

Traditional Blocks

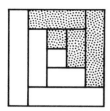

Make 4 blocks.
1/2 white, 1/2 blues
(boy's collar, girl's bonnet)

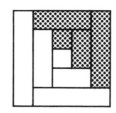

Make 4 blocks.
1/2 white, 1/2 browns
(girl's collar and hair)

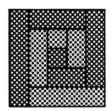

Make 4 blocks.
Browns with black
(girl's curls)

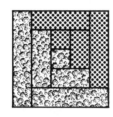

Make 2 blocks.
1/2 bright pink, 1/2 browns
(girl's hair and cheeks)

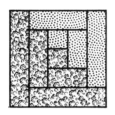

Make 2 blocks.
1/2 bright pink, 1/2 blues
(boy's cheeks and sky)

3. Sew the 70 blocks together as indicated on diagram.

4. Add 2 side strips of 1" wide blue fabric. Add a top strip of 1" wide blue fabric.

5. Now add borders (4" wide brown strips). Borders may be mitered or added a strip at a time: first the two sides, then top and bottom.

6. Applique boy's eye in place. Use brown outline stitch around eye and for eyelashes. Embroider a white satin stitch to indicate gleam.

7. Complete embroidery:

a. noses - dark pink outline stitch

b. mouths - brown outline stitch

c. eyelashes - brown outline stitch (2 or more parallel rows)

d. line between hands - brown outline stitch down the center of hands. Separate the line at the bottom as shown.

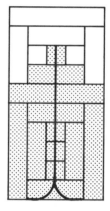

Note: Embroider scroll on large piece of white fabric before cutting out to applique.

8. Add details by stitching notions to wall hanging:
a. buttons on boy's cuffs
b. yellow bow to girl's neck
c. lace to girl's cuffs

9. Mark top for quilting. Quilting suggestion: Outline the figures, hands, and cheeks; then continue the outline at 1" wide intervals.

10. Layer the quilt top, batting, and backing. Quilt through all three layers. Bind edges with 1 1/2" wide strips of beige. (See finishing instructions on page 75.)

Turkey Placemat

Approximate Size: 16" x 16"
(Color photo on page 46)

Color Key

☐ - Beiges

▨ - Dark browns

⬚ - Orange

▨ - Rust

Turkey Placemat and Napkin

Size: 16" x 16"
25 blocks (9-piece blocks)

Materials: 45" wide fabrics
Note: Amounts are for one placemat and napkin only. Multiply yardage by the number of mats and napkins desired.
1/3 yd. assorted dark brown prints for turkey, border, and binding
1/2 yd. assorted beige prints for background
1/4 yd. rust print for border and feathers
1/8 yd. orange print for pumpkins, legs, and feathers
1/8 yd. gold solid for turkey's head
1/8 yd. red print for feathers and wattle
1/8 yd. yellow print for corn and feathers
1/8 yd. green print for leaf and corn husk
1/2 yd. coordinating fabric for backing
Napkins - 15" square per napkin

Notions:
Thread
Embroidery floss - black, brown, white
16" x 19" batting

Directions:
1. Color in the graphs and blocks with colored pencils. This will help eliminate mistakes.
2. Using either the speed-piecing method or the templates, make the following blocks:

Note: For more placemats, multiply the number of each block needed by the number of placemats desired.

Courthouse Steps Blocks

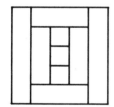

Make 14 blocks.
All beiges (background)

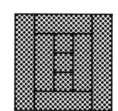

Make 5 blocks.
All browns (turkey)

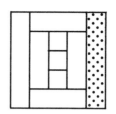

Make 2 blocks.
Beiges with one outside
orange strip (legs)

Traditional Blocks

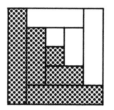

Make 4 blocks.
1/2 browns, 1/2 beiges
(turkey and background)

3. Sew the 25 blocks together as graph indicates.
4. Sew a 1" wide border of brown to all four sides. Sew a 2" wide border of rust to all four sides.
5. Complete applique:
   a. Applique feathers to the turkey's body.
   b. Applique wattle, head, and beak to turkey.
   c. Applique pumpkin to background; add stem and leaf.
   d. Applique corn and corn husk to background.
6. Embroider details:
   a. Lines of pumpkin and leaf stem are in brown outline stitch.
   b. Turkey's eyes are as applique/embroidery sheet indicates.
   c. Turkey's feet are in brown outline stitch.
7. Mark placemat top as desired for quilting. Quilting suggestion: Quilt around turkey, pumpkin, and corn and along borders.
8. Finish as a placemat, using directions on page 79.

Napkin
9. Finish napkins using directions on page 79.

Indian Corn Wall Hanging

Approximate Size: 24" x 34"
(Color photo on page 47)

Color Key

 - Red

 - Deep red

 - Dark brown

 - Medium brown

 - Beige

Indian Corn Wall Hanging

Size: 24" x 34"
15 blocks (9-piece blocks)

Materials: 45" wide fabric
5/8 yd. muslin or off-white fabric for background
1/3 yd. assorted dark brown fabrics for leaves, corn, and outer border
1/4 yd. medium brown print for leaves, corn, and second border
1/4 yd. beige solid for leaves and corn
1/8 yd. red print for bow and ribbon
1/3 yd. deep red solid for inner bow, ribbon, border, binding, and corn
Scraps of yellows, golds, rusts, reds for corn
2/3 yd. coordinating backing fabric

Notions:
Threads
Batting, binding, and thread to finish

Note: Sample shown is machine appliqued. If you wish to hand applique and embroider, add the following to notions list:
Embroidery floss
Dark brown for leaf veins
Dark red to outline inner bow

Directions:
1. The blocks for this design have colors chosen randomly as they are sewn, so there is no need to color the blocks with colored pencils.
2. Using either the speed-piecing method or the templates, make the following blocks:

Courthouse Steps Blocks

Make 15 blocks.

Fabrics should be placed randomly in each block for a more "natural" corn appearance. Use reds, browns, golds, rusts, beiges, and yellows.
3. When the 15 blocks are completed, sew together in 3 linear strips of 5 blocks each. Make 3 strips like this.

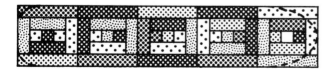

4. Trim ends to corn shape, making one end slightly more pointed.
5. Reread machine applique instructions before cutting fabric pieces.
6. After fabrics are prepared and cut, prepare a background piece of muslin or off-white fabric. Cut a rectangle 19" x 29".

7. Lay fabrics on background as illustrated. (Mark background with pencil or water-soluble fabric marking pen, if desired.) Pieces should be layered and applied in the following order:

    a. Red ribbon sash (piece #9) - use red thread
    b. Middle corn ear
    c. Left corn ear - use gold, brown, or red thread
    d. Right corn ear
    e. Beige leaf (#5)
    f. Dark brown leaf (#6)
    g. Medium brown leaves (#1, 4, and 7) - use beige thread for leaves
    h. Beige leaf (#3)
    i. Dark brown leaf (#2)
    j. Deep red ribbon (#8) Be careful to make it go over leaf #1 and appear to go behind left corn ear.
    k. Red ribbon (#10) and deep red ribbon #11
    l. Red bow
    m. Deep red portions of inner bow

8. Machine embroider leaf veins in dark brown satin stitch. (Use beige thread on dark leaves.)
9. Add borders:

    a. Deep red border - cut strips 1 1/4" wide

    b. Medium brown border - cut strips 1" wide

    c. Dark brown border - cut strips 2" wide

10. Mark quilt top as desired for quilting. Quilting suggestion: Outline corn and leaves, then quilt a cross-hatched grid across the background (diagonal lines spaced 1" apart).

11. Layer quilt top, batting, and backing. Quilt through all three layers. Bind edges using 1" wide strips of deep red. (See finishing instructions on page 75.)

Creative Option: Sample shown is machine appliqued. If you wish to hand applique, it will be necessary to make larger blocks so that you will have a seam allowance to fold under. Follow the directions given, except make 13-piece blocks instead of 9-piece blocks for the corn. Be sure to add seam allowances to ribbon and leaf templates.

Jolly Santa Wall Hanging

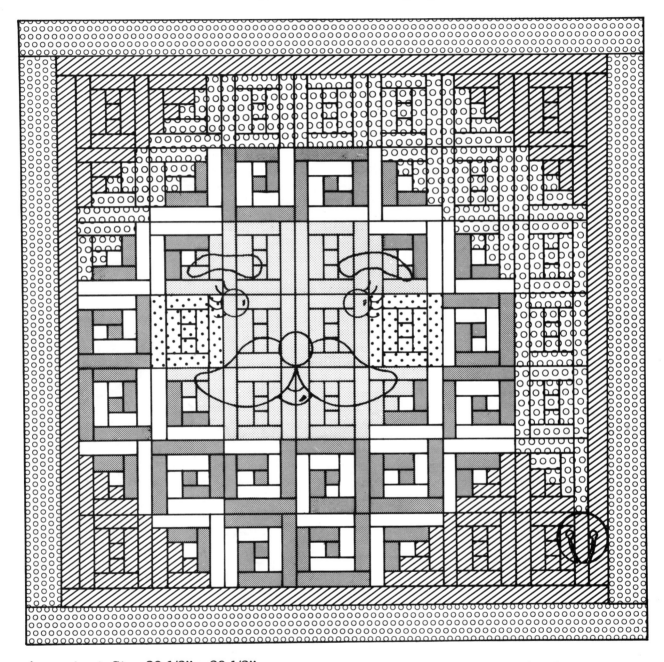

Approximate Size: 20 1/2'' x 20 1/2''
(Color photo on page 48)

Color Key

- Red
- White
- Green
- Gray
- Pink
- Flesh

Christmas

The Christmas tree is probably the most time-honored of all Christmas traditions. In our house, we have a special tree in the family room for heart-shaped ornaments only. Each year a few new ones are added to the collection. A second tree in the living room is for all the favorite decorations collected and made over the years, including those my daughters made when they were growing up.

One of my favorite family traditions is the stocking presents — small, inexpensive gifts we exchange on Christmas Eve. The Snowman and Reindeer stockings I've included in this section are large, allowing Santa to be generous.

I have used the wreath design included here for several different projects. Each wreath is the right size for a placemat. I also have made this design in a large Christmas quilt, door quilt, pillow, and wall hanging.

Jolly Santa Wall Hanging

Size: 20 1/2" x 20 1/2"
49 blocks (9-piece blocks)

Materials: 45" wide fabrics
3/8 yd. flesh fabric for face
3/8 yd. white fabric for beard, moustache, and eyebrows
3/8 yd. light gray fabric for beard
3/8 yd. total assorted green fabrics for background
1/2 yd. total assorted red fabric for hat, border, and lips
1/8 yd. pink fabric for cheeks
Small piece of blue fabric for eyes
Small piece of gold fabric for jingle bell
Small piece of dark pink fabric for nose
5/8 yd. fabric for backing

Notions:
White embroidery floss
Black embroidery floss
Batting, binding, and thread to finish

Directions:

1. Color in the graphs and blocks with colored pencils. This will help eliminate mistakes.

2. Using either the speed-piecing method or the templates, make the following blocks:

Courthouse Steps Blocks

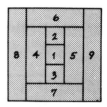

Make 2 blocks.
All pink

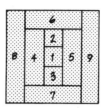

Make 6 blocks.
All flesh

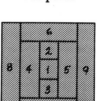

Make 5 blocks.
Assorted greens

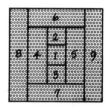

Make 7 blocks.
Assorted reds

Traditional Blocks

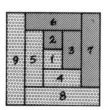

Make 5 blocks.
1/2 green, 1/2 red

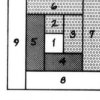

Make 4 blocks.
1/2 red,
1/2 gray and white

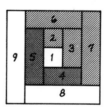

Make 4 blocks.
1/2 green,
1/2 gray and white

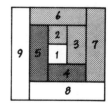

Make 4 blocks.
1/2 flesh,
1/2 gray and white

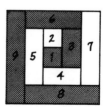

Make 12 blocks.
Spiraled gray and white

3. Sew the 49 blocks together as indicated on graph.

4. Sew 1" wide green strip to each of the four sides.

5. Now add borders (2" wide red strips). Borders may be mitered or added a strip at a time: first, the two sides, then top and bottom.

6. Complete applique using patterns on this page.

    a. eyes and eyebrows, lips

    b. moustache overlaps lips

    c. nose overlaps moustache

    d. jingle bell

7. Add embroidery:

    a. Embroider around eyes and jingle bell in black outline stitch.

    b. Embroider eyelashes in black outline stitch.

    c. Embroider reflection in eyes and on lips in white satin stitch.

8. Mark top for quilting. Quilting suggestion: Outline face, eyebrows, eyes, nose, mouth, and moustache. Outline hair, hat, and jingle bell.

9. Layer the top, batting, and backing. Quilt through all three layers. Bind edges with 1 1/2" wide strips of red. See finishing instructions on page 75.

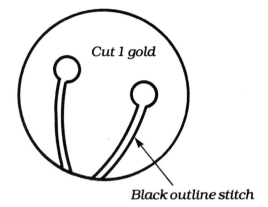

Cut 1 gold

Black outline stitch

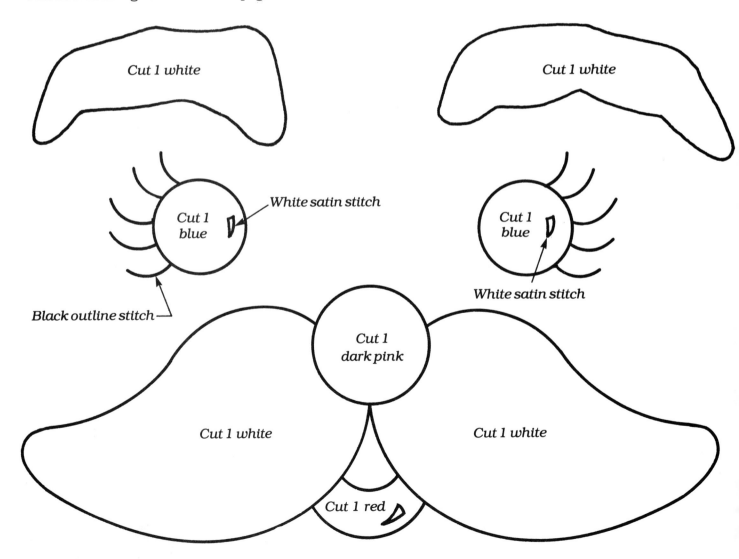

Cut 1 white

Cut 1 white

White satin stitch

Cut 1 blue

Cut 1 blue

White satin stitch

Black outline stitch

Cut 1 dark pink

Cut 1 white

Cut 1 white

Cut 1 red

Snowman Stocking

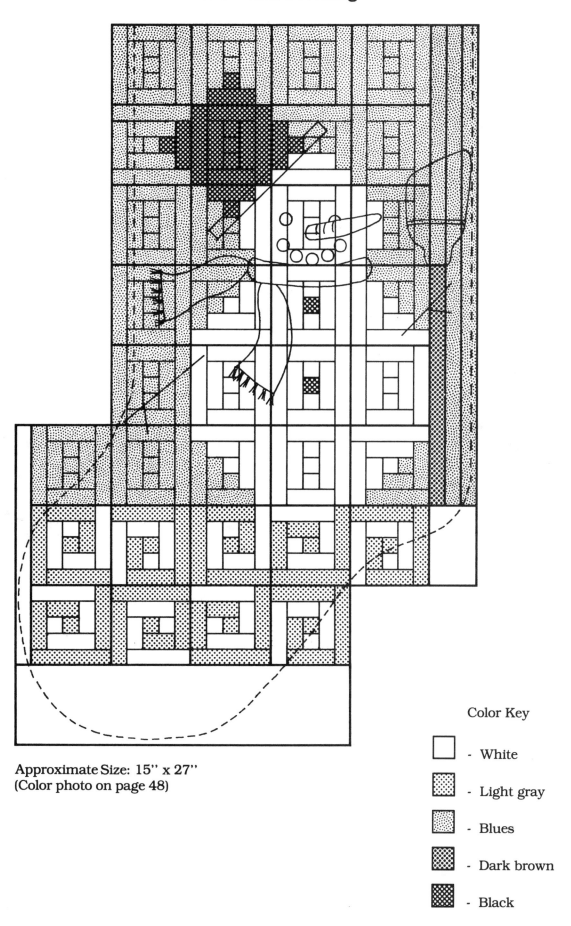

Approximate Size: 15" x 27"
(Color photo on page 48)

Color Key

☐ - White

▨ - Light gray

▨ - Blues

▨ - Dark brown

▨ - Black

Snowman Stocking

Size: 15" x 27"
34 blocks (9-piece blocks)

Materials: 45" wide fabric
1/2 yd. medium blues
3 yds. white fabric for pieced front, stocking back,
  lining, cuff, and backing
1/8 yd. light gray solid for snow swirls
1/8 yd. black for hat, buttons
1/8 yd. red print for muffler, holly, cuff band
1/8 yd. brown print for broom handle
1/8 yd. gold for broom
1/2 yd. assorted green fabrics for holly leaves and
  bias binding
1/8 yd. orange fabric for nose

Notions:
3 yds. cable cord to make stocking cording
2 yds. 3/8" wide green grosgrain ribbon
2 yds. 3/8" wide red grosgrain ribbon
2 large gold jingle bells
Metal or plastic ring to hang stocking
Embroidery floss: brown, blue, black, red
17" x 30" batting
Thread

Directions:
1. Color in the graph and blocks with colored pencils.
This will help eliminate mistakes.

2. Using either the speed-piecing method or the templates, make the following blocks:

Courthouse Steps Blocks

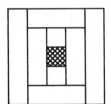

Make 9 blocks.
All blues (sky)

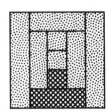

Make 4 blocks.
All white (snowman)

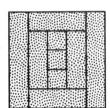

Make 2 blocks.
White with a
black center
(snowman and buttons)

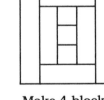

Make 2 blocks.
Blues with black
(sky and hat)

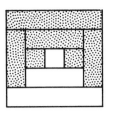

Make 1 block.
Blues and white
(snowman's head)

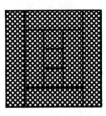

Make 1 block.
Black (hat)

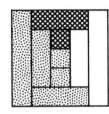

Make 1 block.
Blues, black, and white
(head, hat, and sky)

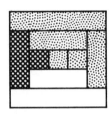

Make 1 block.
Blues, black, and white
(head, hat, and sky)

Traditional Blocks

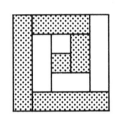

Make 9 blocks.
Light gray and white
(snow swirls)

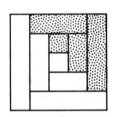

Make 4 blocks.
1/2 white, 1/2 blues
(snowman and sky)

MARY EMMERLING AND CHRIS MEAD
AMERICAN COUNTRY CHRISTMAS

Everyone who can goes home for Christmas, and the heart's home in the American tradition is the country—"those happy ways where once we went," the idealized past. In a new book, interior designer Mary Emmerling and photographer Chris Mead show homes decorated in the classic country spirit. Above: When they lived in a New York City loft, Mary and her children hung their stockings on an antique herb rack like this one; beneath it are baskets of candy and nuts for visiting friends.

MORE ▶

3. Assemble the blocks containing the sky and snow-man. Cut these side strips:

    Brown - 1" x 8"

    Blue - 1" x 8"

    Blue - 2 strips - 1" x 15 1/2"

Sew the brown strip to the short blue strip to form a linear strip 1" x 15 1/2".

4. Sew this to the other 2 blue strips and attach all 3 to the right-hand side of snowman as shown. This forms the broom handle and additional sky area.

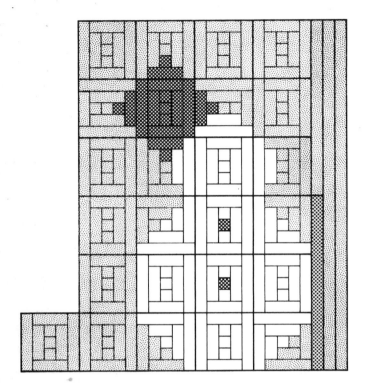

5. Now, assemble the 9 "Snow Swirl" blocks as shown. Add a piece of white 3" x 2". Sew this section to the snowman section as picture graph indicates.

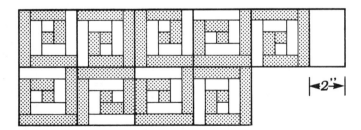

6. After "Swirl" section is added, add a 1" wide strip of white to the left side.

7. Now, add a strip of white (3" wide) to the bottom. This extra piecing eliminates the need to make additional pieced blocks, which would be cut away anyway.

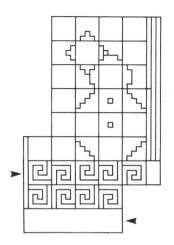

Add 1" wide white side strip and 3" wide bottom strip

8. Complete applique:

    a. Brim of top hat - black fabric

    b. Top of broom - gold fabric

    c. Carrot nose - orange fabric

    d. Muffler around neck - red fabric

    e. Holly leaves - green fabric

9. Embroider details:

    a. "Coal" eyes and mouth - black satin stitch

    b. Lines in carrot - brown outline stitch

    c. "Stick" arms - several rows of brown outline stitch

    d. Vertical lines in broom - brown outline stitch

    e. Broom bands - blue outline stitch

    f. Veins in holly leaves - black outline stitch

    g. Holly berries - red satin stitch

    h. Muffler fringe - red satin stitch and outline stitch

Assembly:

1. Cut out the stocking, following the broken lines on the diagram. Layer the stocking for quilting with polyester batting and white fabric backing as shown. Hand or machine quilt as desired.

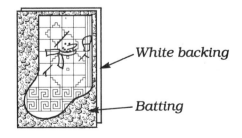

White backing

Batting

2. When stocking front is quilted, trim batting and backing to match stocking front.

3. To make cording, cut bias strips, 1 1/2" wide, from green fabric. Piece these together to form a strip 3 yds. long. Then, using a zipper foot, fold fabric around purchased cable cord and stitch to form cording.

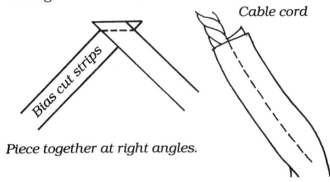

Cable cord

Bias cut strips

Piece together at right angles.

Cable cord

1. Placing raw edges together, sew cording to stocking front with zipper foot. With right sides together, place stocking front next to a rectangular piece of white fabric. Still using the zipper foot, sew stocking front to back along cording stitches. Trim white back to match front. Clip curves to stitching and turn stocking right side out.

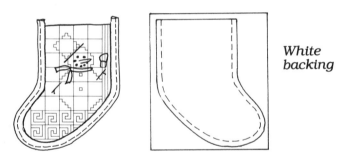

White backing

2. Using stocking front as a pattern, cut 2 linings from white fabric. Place right sides together and sew around seams, leaving top open. Make seam allowances slightly larger than stocking seams, so the lining will fit inside. Note: Quilting the stocking front will "shrink" it somewhat, so the lining may have to be adjusted accordingly.

3. Do not turn lining to right side, but slip lining into the quilted stocking. Sew stocking to lining along top edge as shown.

Lining

Stocking Cuff

1. To cut cuff, measure the top of stocking front. Double this measurement and add 3". For example, if your stocking front measures 12", double that (24") and add 3" (27").

2. Cut a piece of white fabric 27" long (or your measurement) and 6" wide. Add a 2" wide strip of red fabric to the bottom. Position the name and holly leaves on the right only, at least 2" in from edge. Mark as desired, for quilting. Add batting and white backing and quilt the entire cuff section.

Leave 2" to right of holly.

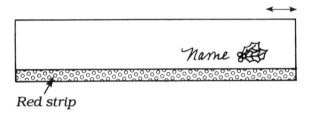

Name

Red strip

3. With raw edges out and using a zipper foot, sew the remaining length of green cording to the top of quilted cuff.

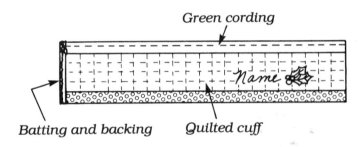

Green cording

Name

Batting and backing   *Quilted cuff*

4. Now cut a facing the same size as cuff. With right sides together, and still using the zipper foot, sew lining to cuff along cording stitches.

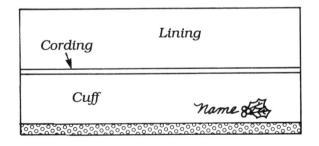

Lining

Cording

Cuff   *Name*

66

5. Fold cuff and lining in half, right sides together as shown, and stitch along edge.

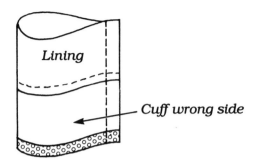
Lining

Cuff wrong side

6. With right sides together, sew cuff to top of stocking along top edge. Turn cuff lining to inside and hem.

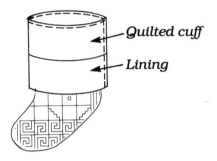
Quilted cuff

Lining

Finishing

Thread a jingle bell through a 24" length of green ribbon. Thread a jingle bell through a 30" length of red ribbon. Tie bows with each of the remaining pieces of red and green ribbon. Attach bells and bows to upper right-hand corner of stocking. Sew on a metal or plastic ring.

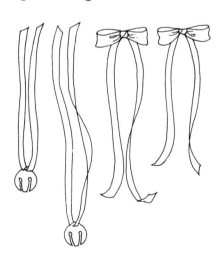

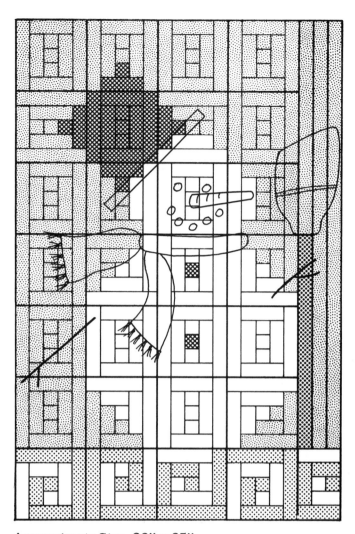

Approximate Size: 20" x 25"

Snowman Wall Hanging

You may choose to rearrange the blocks and finish your snowman as a wall hanging.

1. You will only need to make 29 blocks. Make all of the blocks in the same amounts except for the blue background blocks (make 8 instead of 9) and the light gray and white "Snow Swirl" blocks (make 5 instead of 9).

2. Assemble the blocks containing the sky and snowman. Cut and add the side- strips following direction 3 on page 65.

3. Add the 5 "Snow Swirl" blocks beneath the sky and snowman sections as shown in diagram.

4. Add 2" wide white border to all four sides.

5. Add a 3" wide blue border to all four sides. Miter corners if desired.

6. Follow directions given under stocking to complete applique and embroidery.

7. Mark wall hanging for quilting as desired. Layer quilt top with batting and backing and quilt through all three layers. Bind edges with 1 1/2" wide strips of blue fabric. (See finishing instructions on page 75.)

Reindeer Stocking

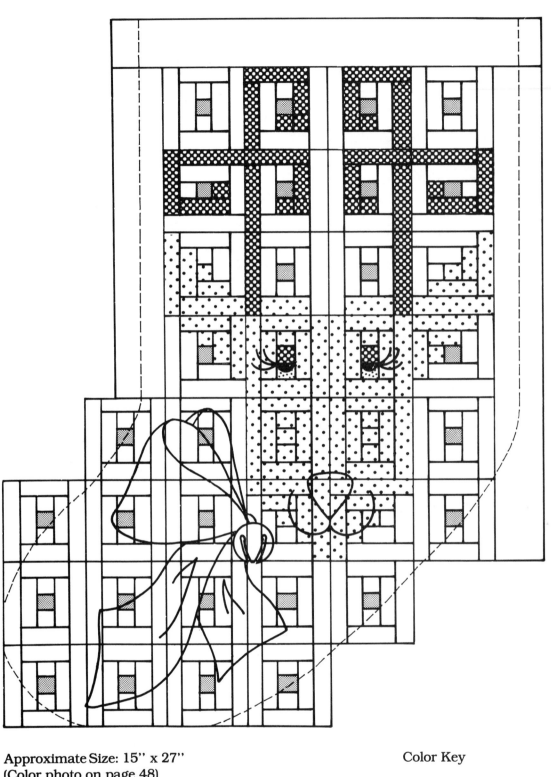

Approximate Size: 15" x 27"
(Color photo on page 48)

Color Key

- Brown

- Dark brown

- Green

- Blue

- White

68

Reindeer Stocking

Size: Stocking is 15" x 27"
      Wall Hanging is 18 1/2" x 30"
36 blocks (9-piece blocks)

Materials: 45" wide fabrics
3 yds. white for pieced front, back, lining, cuff, and backing
1/8 yd. bright red for bow, holly berries, and cuff band
1/2 yd. green for holly leaf, stocking front piecing, and bias strips for stocking cording
1/4 yd. total of 3 similar medium browns for reindeer
1/16 yd. of dark brown for antlers and eyelids
Small pieces of the following:
    black for nose
    gold for jingle bell
    blue for eyes
    dark red for bow
    dark green for holly leaf
3 yds. cotton cable cord to make stocking cording
2 yds. green ribbon (3/8" wide)
2 yds. red ribbon (3/8" wide)
2 large gold jingle bells
Metal or plastic ring to hang stocking
Embroidery floss: black and white
19" x 32" batting

Directions:

1. Color in the graph and blocks with colored pencils. This will help eliminate mistakes.

2. Using either the speed-piecing method or the templates, make the following blocks:

Courthouse Steps Blocks

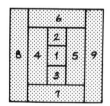

Make 2 blocks.
All brown (reindeer)

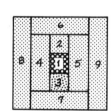

Make 2 blocks.
Brown with black and blue (eyes)

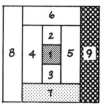

Make 1 block.
White, green, browns (antlers)

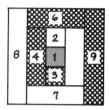

Make 1 block.
White, greens, browns (antlers)

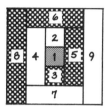

Make 3 blocks.
White, greens, browns (antlers)

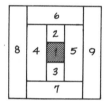

Make 3 blocks.
White, green, browns (antlers)

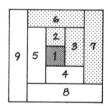

Make 18 blocks.
White with green (background)

Traditional Blocks

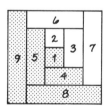

Make 4 blocks.
Medium brown and white

Make 2 blocks.
Green center with medium brown and white

69

3. Assemble the blocks for reindeer as shown below. You will need 3 strips of white fabric, 1 1/2" wide by approximately 15" long. These are sewn to the sides and top of the blocks in the order shown.

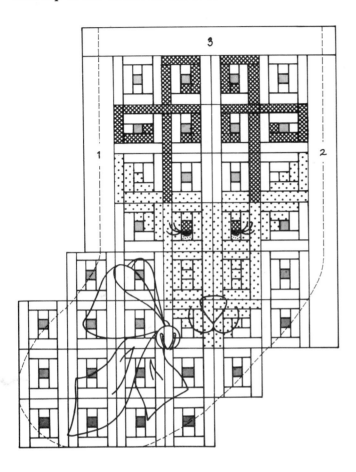

4. Complete applique:

   a. nose - black fabric

   b. bow - 2 shades of red fabric as shown in color photograph on page 48.

   c. jingle bell - gold fabric

5. Embroider details:

   a. eyes - black semicircle in satin stitch on the blue eye and below the eyelid as shown on picture

   b. eyelashes - black outline stitch

   c. mouth - black outline stitch

   d. lines on bow and jingle bell - black outline stitch

   e. reflection on nose and eyes - white satin stitch

6. Finish as a stocking, following directions for Snowman Stocking on pages 65-67.

Reindeer Wall Hanging

Approximate Size: 18 1/2" x 30"

You may choose to rearrange the blocks and finish as a wall hanging.

Assemble blocks as shown below. You will also need 2 strips of white fabric, 2" x 23" and 2 strips of white fabric, 2" x 10 1/2". You will need 2 strips of red fabric 2" x 26" and 2 strips of red fabric 2" x 14" for borders. These are sewn to blocks in the order shown.

1. Assemble the blocks in horizontal rows first.

2. Then, matching seams, sew the eight rows together to form the complete picture.

3. Sew white strips to sides, then to top and bottom.

4. Sew red strips to sides, then to top and bottom.

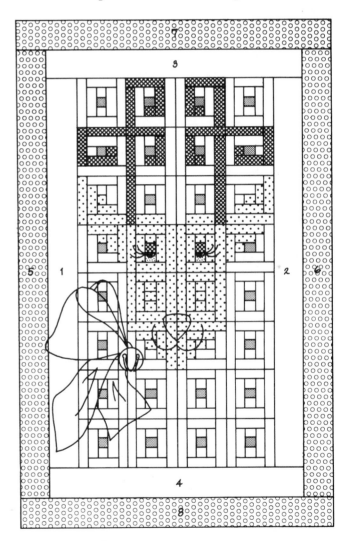

5. Follow directions given under stocking to complete applique and embroidery.

6. Mark wall hanging for quilting as desired. Layer quilt top with batting and backing and quilt through all three layers. Bind edges with 1 1/2" wide strips of blue fabric. (See finishing instructions on page 75.)

Christmas Wreath Table Runner

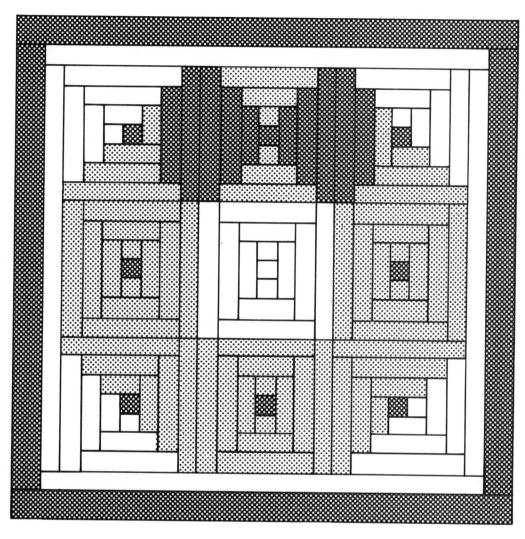

Approximate Size: 15" wide
(length determined by your table length)
(Color photo on page 47)

Color Key

☐ - White

▨ - Greens

▩ - Red

Christmas Wreath Table Runner

Size: 15" wide (length depends on table)
18 blocks (13-piece blocks)
2 wreaths of 9 blocks each

Materials: 45" wide fabric
1 yd. white solid fabric for background and center strip
3/4 yd. assorted dark green prints for wreaths and binding (includes 1/4 yd. of one green for binding)
1/4 yd. red solid for bows and berries
1 yd. backing fabric
168" of a 2-3" wide Christmas border print cut from striped fabric. (Determine number of repeats in 1 yd. and compute accordingly.)

Notions:
Thread
Batting
2 yds. red or green decorative (braided) cord

Directions:
1. Color in the picture graph and blocks with colored pencils. This will help eliminate mistakes.
2. Using either the speed-piecing method or the templates, make the following blocks:

Courthouse Steps Blocks

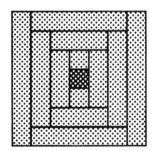

Make 6 blocks.
Greens with red center
(wreath and berry)

Make 2 blocks.
Red and greens
(bow)

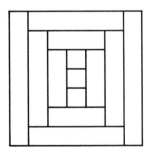

Make 2 blocks.
Whites
(center of wreath)

Traditional Blocks

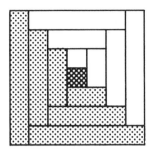

Make 4 blocks.
Red center with
greens and white
(corners of wreath)

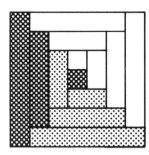

Make 2 blocks.
Red center with
greens, red, and white
(bow & wreath)

Full-Size Templates

* special piecing

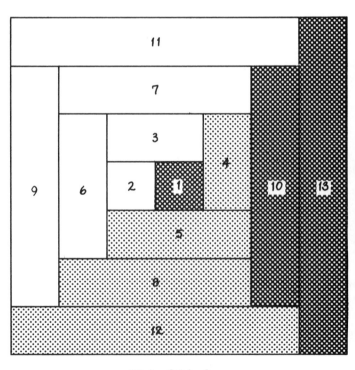

Make 2 blocks.
Red center with
greens, red, and white
(bow & wreath)

3. Assemble the wreaths as illustrated.

4. Add strips of 1" wide white fabric to all four sides.

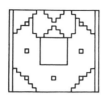

5. Measure your wreath from top to bottom. It should measure approximately 11 1/2". Double this measurement and subtract this from the table length measurement.

Example:

Table length measures	60"
less 2 wreath	
measurements (2 x 11 1/2")	– 23"
Cut center section (white)	37"

Your measurements:
Your table length _____
less your wreath x 2 – _____
Cut center fabric section _____

6. Sew this piece between 2 wreaths.

7. Cut 2 pieces of white fabric 12 1/2" x 5 1/2". Fold each in half and draw a line as indicated. Cut on line.

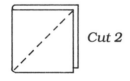

Cut 2

8. Sew the resulting large triangles to each end of runner.
Note: This triangle will hang over ends of table.

9. Cut 2 1/2" wide strips for border. This may be varied as the width of your border design fabric indicates. Miter corners.

10. Plan a quilting design to fit the size of your white center. There are many Christmas quilting designs available. Quilting suggestion: Quilt snowflake design in center section, quilt around wreaths and in triangle sections.

11. After marking quilting lines, layer the runner top, batting, and backing. Quilt through all three layers. Bind edges using 1 1/2" wide green strips. (See finishing instructions on page 75.)

12. Cut braided cord in half.

13. Tie 2 bows from braided cord and sew to the tips of triangle sections.

Creative Option: A single wreath motif as pictured on page 49 may be made and used in a placemat, pillow, or as a wall hanging. (See finishing instructions for placemat on page 79, pillow on page 77, or wall hanging on pages 74-75.)

A pattern for an applique mouse is found on the large pattern sheet. Mouse can rest in the middle of wreath. Use black embroidery floss to embroider details.

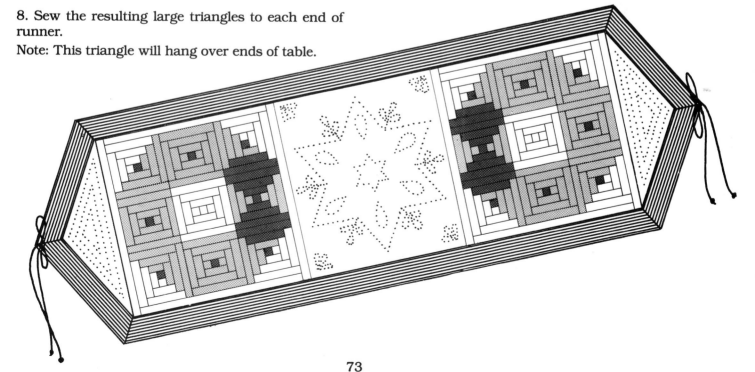

Finishing Techniques

Most of the projects in this book can be finished in a variety of ways. The project directions and photographs usually suggest only one finishing technique. However, you can adapt each pieced project to another end use. All of the wall hangings can be mounted on stretcher bar frames and vice versa. The smaller pieced motifs (ranging from 14" to 18") can be used interchangeably in pillows, placemats, or tote bags. Even the motifs on the Christmas stockings can be adapted to a rectangular shape and made into a wall hanging.

Wall Hangings and Quilts

Adding Borders

Borders may be added a strip at a time, or strips for borders may be sewn together and then mitered.

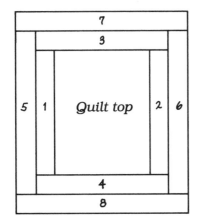

Add borders in numerical order. It is like a giant Courthouse Steps block.

Mitered Borders

1. Mark the center edges of the borders and design area by folding them in half and inserting a pin at the fold.

2. With right sides together, match borders according to diagrams. Pin in place at beginning and end of seam line. Be sure to match center pins.

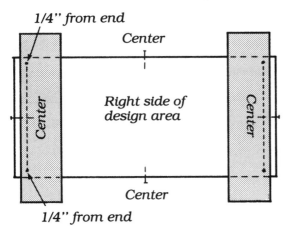

3. Baste and stitch two opposite borders in place, beginning and ending seams 1/4" from ends.

4. Press seams flat with seam allowances toward the borders.

5. Repeat with remaining two borders. (Seams will all begin and end at the ends of the two previously stitched border seams.) Anchor these points with a pin.

6. Working on one corner at a time, fold top border under to form a mitered corner.

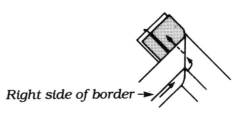

7. Align seam lines of border strips (see arrows). Pin as shown. Press fold, remove pins, and press a firm crease at fold.

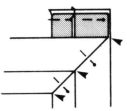

8. Leave pins in borders as shown in diagram.

9. Fold borders with right sides together. Open seams and fold away from border. Insert pins through edges of border strips. Check underneath to see if pins are aligned with seams and adjust pins if necessary.

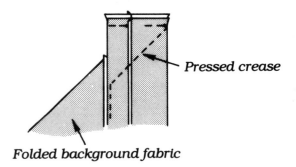

10. Baste pressed crease. Stitch on basting outward from design area to border edges. Remove basting. Trim 1/4" away from seam.

Preparing to Quilt

1. Cut out quilt backing and batting, using front of wall hanging as a cutting guide and allowing extra backing and batting to extend at least 1" beyond front.

2. Position batting on top of backing. Place wall hanging on top of batting. Baste all three layers together from the center to the outside corners and edges. Baste outer edges.

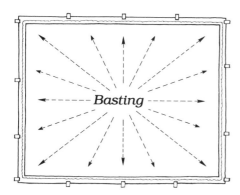

Quilting

Suggestions for placement of quilting are given with each project. To quilt by hand, you will need quilting thread, quilting needles, small scissors, a thimble, and maybe a balloon or large rubber band to help grasp the needle if it gets stuck. Quilt on a frame, a large hoop, or just on a table or your lap. Use a single thread no longer than 18". Make a small, single knot in the end of the thread. The quilting stitch is a small, running stitch that goes through all three layers of the quilt. To begin, insert the needle in the top layer about 3/4" from the point you want to start stitching. Pull the needle out at the starting point and gently tug at the knot until it pops through the fabric and is buried in the batting. Make a small backstitch through all three layers at the beginning of the quilting line. Proceed to quilt with small, even stitches until coming almost to the end of the thread. There, make a single knot fairly close to the fabric. Make a backstitch to bury the knot in the batting. Run the thread off through the batting and out the quilt top, and snip it off. Repeat until the whole quilt is quilted.

Hand quilting stitch

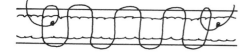

Binding

There are numerous ways to finish the edges of a quilt. For the patterns in this book, I have used self-made binding strips. Strips are sewn, one at a time, to sides, top, and bottom of quilt through all three layers (quilt top, batting, and backing). This can be done by hand or machine. Strips are then folded to the backing and stitched down by hand.

1. Stitch along edges through all layers.

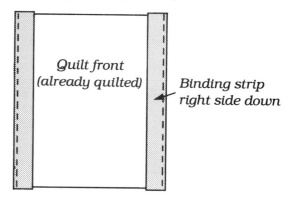

2. Open side bindings before sewing on top and bottom binding strips.

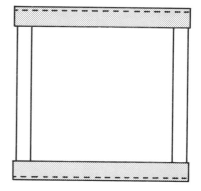

3. Fold binding strips to back and stitch by hand.

Square the corners or miter corners.

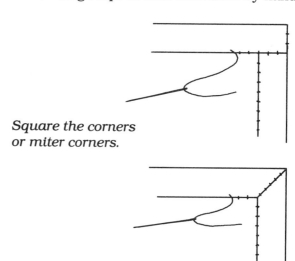

Casings for Rods

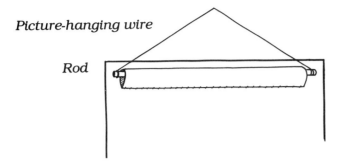

Picture-hanging wire

Rod

Casings are linear fabric tubes, attached by hand to the finished quilt. These often are required in quilt shows with varying size requirements. Make a tube almost the width of the finished quilt, hemming the ends. As you attach it to the quilt, make sure to stitch down the sides so that a rod cannot be inadvertently slid against the quilt itself, causing damage.

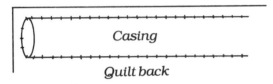

Casing

Quilt back

Stretcher Bar Frames

Purchase stretcher bars approximately 3" smaller than the finished wall hanging. Assemble the wooden stretcher bar frame according to manufacturer's directions, checking the corners with a right angle to make sure they are square. Staple a layer of prewashed muslin over the stretcher bar frame to keep the wall hanging from coming in contact with the wood.

Place stretcher bar over right side of quilt to determine position. Make a dot in each corner to indicate proper position of frame.

Place frame on floor or table. Place quilt over stretcher bars, aligning positioning dot with corner of frame. To hold the quilt in place for stapling, use push pins along the outside edge of the frame. Don't stretch or pull quilt wall hanging too tightly, as the seam lines will become distorted.

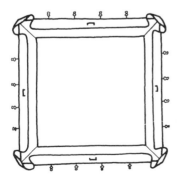

Carefully turn stretcher bar frame over, making sure you do not dislodge the push pins. Begin stapling quilt to frame by placing one staple in the middle of each side. On one side, work from the center out, inserting staples 2" to 3" apart and stopping 2" from each corner. Staple the opposite side, then the other two sides.

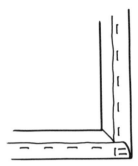

Finish corners by neatly folding into place. Remove push pins. Finish back by covering raw edges with a muslin square. Attach eye screws and picture-hanging wire.

Muslin

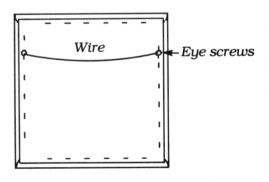

Wire ← *Eye screws*

Corded Pillows

1. Cut 1 1/2" wide strips of fabric to make cording. (This need not be cut on the bias). Piece the strips together to form a length of 70" (or longer if pillow form is larger than 16" x 16").

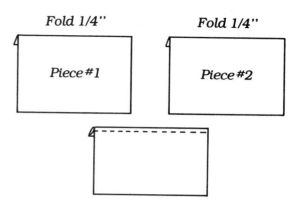

Fold 1/4"   *Fold 1/4"*

Piece #1   *Piece #2*

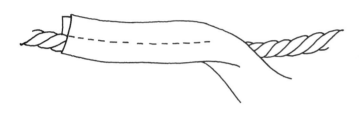

Piece strip where necessary.

2. Use a zipper foot to make cording. Wrap fabric strip around cord as you sew and stitch with machine close to cord.

2. Overlap the two pieces, with hemmed edges toward each other, so that there is a 6" overlap and the resulting square is 17" x 17". Note: If making a larger pillow, adjust sizes accordingly.

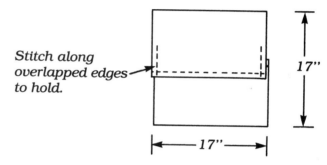

Stitch along overlapped edges to hold.

17"

17"

3. Now stitch cording to pillow front, still using zipper foot. Gently round the corners as you sew and clip cording at curves.

3. Place pillow back and corded pillow front with right sides together.

4. Following stitching on pillow front and still using the zipper foot, sew front to back all the way around pillow.

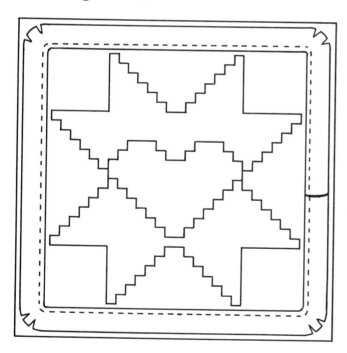

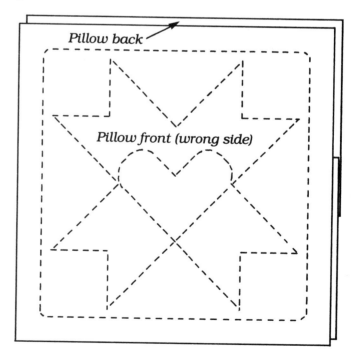

Pillow back

Pillow front (wrong side)

For pillow back with a "slit" opening:

1. Cut 2 pieces of backing fabric 17" x 12". Fold 1/4" seam allowance along one 17" side of each piece. Press. Fold another 1/4". Press. Stitch closely along folded edge. Hem each piece along one long edge.

5. Trim seam allowances and turn pillow to right side. Insert pillow form through back slit.

Trick-or-Treat Bag

1. Sew 2" wide strips of orange fabric to all four sides of pieced block. Cut a backing piece of fabric and a piece of polyester batting a little larger than motif section. This backing fabric will not show, but will be a backing for quilting the motif. Baste the three layers together and hand or machine quilt. Quilting suggestion: Outline outside of motif, then any details.

Backing

Batting

2. Cut a bag back the same size as the quilted bag front. With right sides together, stitch front to back along sides and bottom, using 1/2" seam allowances. Turn bag to right side.

3. Cut 2 handles 20" long by 4 1/2" wide. Press interfacing to wrong side of strips. Fold handles in half lengthwise, right sides together. Stitch along raw edges as shown, leaving ends open. Then, using a safety pin or turning tool, turn handles to right side. Press. Topstitch along the length of handles, 1/4" from edge.

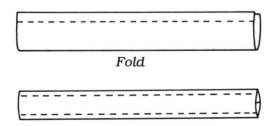

Fold

*Turn to right side
and topstitch along edges.*

4. Sew handles to bag with raw edges up, one handle to quilted cat front, one handle to bag back, as shown.

5. Measure the finished bag's width and depth. Add 1" to each of these measurements and cut 2 lining pieces. Using 1/2" seam allowance and with right sides together, sew the lining pieces together at sides and bottom. Do not turn to right side, but slip the lining into the bag and match side seams. Fold raw edges toward each other and slip stitch edges together along top, keeping handles free.

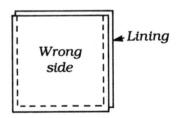

Wrong side

Lining

6. For extra stability, machine stitch through all layers along upper edge.

78

Sweatshirt

Be sure to prewash sweatshirt if it has been purchased. Cut a piece of fusible interfacing 1" longer than pieced block on all sides.

Press interfacing onto inside of sweatshirt front, following manufacturer's instructions. Place it behind the area where you plan to applique. This will eliminate stretching of the sweatshirt as you work.

Now, applique the pieced block to the sweatshirt front by hand or machine.

Placemat

Sew 2" wide strips of coordinating fabric to sides of the pieced block only. Cut batting and backing slightly larger than block section. Baste three layers together and hand or machine quilt. Quilting suggestion: Outline outside of block, then quilt around details. Bind edges of mat with 2" wide strips of coordinating fabric. For a coordinated look, make or purchase matching napkins.

Napkins

Size: 14 1/2" x 14 1/2"

Materials: (Yardage given is for 1 napkin only; multiply the amount by the number of napkins desired.)
1/2 yd. fabric

Directions:

1. Cut a 15" x 15" fabric square for each napkin desired.

2. Fold under 1/4" on all edges and press to wrong side.

3. Fold under 1/4" a second time to cover all raw edges. Press.

4. Stitch along edges.

5. Machine applique mouse or pumpkin to corners as shown in photographs.

About the Author

Having no formal art training, Christal Carter took her first quilting class in 1979. Since then, she has attended many seminars and classes taught by top names in quilting. Her Log Cabin picture designs have won prizes and attracted national attention, appearing in numerous publications. She currently teaches and lectures for groups and guilds nationwide on "Creative Thinking" and "Log Cabin Design".

Christal lives with her businessman husband and two teenage daughters in orange- and avocado-growing country, one hour north of San Diego, in Valley Center, California. Other interests include painting, writing poetry, and working in the Young Life organization as a volunteer adult leader. She has many collections, including antiques, bears, hearts, snails, flags, teapots, and cast-iron cookstoves.

That Patchwork Place Publications

Bearwear by Nancy J. Martin
Branching Out-Tree Quilts by Carolann Palmer
Cathedral Window-A New View by Mary Ryder Kline
Christmas Classics by Sue Saltkill
Christmas Quilts by Marsha McCloskey
Country Christmas by Sue Saltkill
Dozen Variables by M. McCloskey and N. Martin
Feathered Star Quilts by Marsha McCloskey
Feathered Star Sampler by Marsha McCloskey
Housing Projects by Nancy J. Martin
Linens and Old Lace by Nancy Martin and Sue Saltkill
Make a Medallion by Kathy Cook
More Template-Free Quiltmaking by Trudie Hughes
Pieces of the Past by Nancy J. Martin
Projects for Blocks and Borders by Marsha McCloskey
Quilts From A Different Angle by Sara Nephew
Quilter's Christmas by Nancyann Twelker
Sew Special by Susan A. Grosskopf
Small Quilts by Marsha McCloskey
Stencil Patch by Nancy Martin
Template-Free Quiltmaking by Trudie Hughes
Touch of Fragrance by Marine Bumbalough
Wall Quilts by Marsha McCloskey

(Prices subject to change)